Embrace the Undoing

Embrace the Undoing

The Freedom of Grace Enough

Andrea Coli

Embrace the Undoing: The Freedom of Grace Enough

Copyright © 2024 by Andrea Coli

Published in association with Story Architect. www.booksandsuch.com

All rights reserved. No part of this publication may be reproduced, stored in a retrieval system, or transmitted in any form or by any means—electronic, mechanical, photocopy, recording or any other—except for brief quotations in printed reviews without the written prior permission of the publisher.

The website addresses recommended throughout this book are offered as a resource to you. These websites are not intended in any way to be or imply an endorsement on the part of Story Architect, nor do we vouch for their content.

Details in some stories have been changed to protect the identities of the persons involved.

No AI Training. Any use of this publication to "train" artificial intelligence (AI) technologies to generate text is expressly prohibited.

Unless otherwise noted, Scripture quotations are taken from **New International Version.** Scripture quotations marked (NIV) are taken from the Holy Bible, New International Version®, NIV®. Copyright © 1973, 1978, 1984, 2011 by Biblica, Inc.® Used by permission of Zondervan. All rights reserved worldwide. www.zondervan.com The "NIV" and "New International Version" are trademarks registered in the United States Patent and Trademark Office by Biblica, Inc.® Scripture quotations marked (GNT) are from the Good News Translation in Today's English Version- Second Edition Copyright © 1992 by American Bible Society. Used by Permission. Scripture quotations marked MSG are taken from *The Message*, copyright © 1993, 2002, 2018 by Eugene H. Peterson. Used by permission of NavPress. All rights reserved. Represented by Tyndale House Publishers. Scripture quotations taken from the (NASB®) New American Standard Bible®, Copyright © 1960, 1971, 1977, 1995, 2020 by The Lockman Foundation. Used by permission. All rights reserved. lockman.org. Scripture quotations marked (NLT) are taken from the *Holy Bible*, New Living Translation, copyright ©1996, 2004, 2015 by Tyndale House Foundation. Used by permission of Tyndale House Publishers, Carol Stream, Illinois 60188. All rights reserved. Scripture quotations marked TPT are from The Passion Translation®. Copyright © 2017, 2018, 2020 by Passion & Fire Ministries, Inc. Used by permission. All rights reserved. ThePassionTranslation.com. Scripture taken from The Voice™. Copyright © 2012 by Ecclesia Bible Society. Used by permission. All rights reserved. Scripture quotations marked (NIrV) are taken from the Holy BibleNew International Reader's Version®, NIrV® Copyright © 1995, 1996, 1998, 2014 by Biblica, Inc.® Used by permission of Zondervan. All rights reserved worldwide. www.zondervan.com The "NIrV" and "New International Reader's Version" are trademarks registered in the United States Patent and Trademark Office by Biblica, Inc.®

Book Cover by Liana Moisescu

Print ISBN: 978-1-962845-08-3

Printed in the United States of America

For Quinn and Kennedy. Both of you, my girls, are incredibly kind, smart, creative, funny and talented. You have already brought so much to this world, and I know there is more to come. So in the midst of all that, my prayer for you is this: When you are tempted to believe the lie that you must outdo, outshine or outperform for God to be happy with you, you would instead rest easy and live freely in His abundant grace that will never not be enough.

Stuff to Know

You're about to journey through Galatians. This book is designed to be your companion through the rich—and sometimes confusing—early letter by Paul to a church discerning how to live out their faith in Christ. We'll dig into Greek words and Old Testament callbacks that will inspire whatever bit of academic nerd is hiding in you. But it's couched in a conversational way that I hope will feel more like a dialogue among friends. All of that is simply a backdrop to the true purpose behind this book—to spark your own reflection, contemplation, and conversation with God.

The book follows Galatians chronologically. Some chapters here cover a single Bible verse, while others cover an entire chapter.

Galatians is a relatively short letter with only six chapters. It would be helpful to read the entire letter in one sitting before you begin. I recommend doing so in a more conversational version, like The Message or the NLT. If you absolutely love reading and your season of life is such that you can sit for hours without interruption, why not go crazy and read Galatians a few times in different versions? (No shame on those of you who will fully disregard this idea because your only uninterrupted reading happens on your phone in the bathroom. It's all good, friend.)

Speaking of Bible versions, you'll find a number of different versions used throughout this book. As I study and explore the Bible, I find that different versions can often allow the text to be received in fresh ways. That may also be the case with you. Verses included in the book are New International Version unless otherwise noted.

You'll find several reflection questions throughout each chapter. They're designed to help you engage more personally with the text, and to give you space to process what you're reading. Use these prompts in whatever way works best for you. Write as much or as little as you want, and use a separate notebook if desired. The questions aren't seeking right and wrong answers. They're prompts meant to help you listen better to yourself and to God.

Some questions may feel repetitive. That's on purpose, so don't skip over those. The same question on a different day can elicit something completely different or deeper, and God will use those nuances to give you what you need in that moment. Process the questions however fits *you* best. What's most important is that you allow time and mental space to ponder and listen.

I know God is ready for this. Are you? You're embarking on a life-giving journey because that's what God does—leads us on adventures that stretch and grow us!

Table of Contents

Chapter 1 1
Chapter 2 5
Chapter 3 9
Chapter 4 15
Chapter 5 21
Chapter 6 29
Chapter 7 35
Chapter 8 43
Chapter 9 53
Chapter 10 59
Chapter 11 67
Chapter 12 75
Chapter 13 81
Chapter 14 89
Chapter 15 97
Chapter 16 103
Chapter 17 109
Chapter 18 115
Chapter 19 123
Chapter 20 131
Chapter 21 141
Chapter 22 147
Chapter 23 155
Chapter 24 161

Notes 169
A Word of Thanks 171
About the Author 173

Chapter 1

Undone

Let's start off with a confession. (Me, not you.) I'm a bit of a people pleaser. I once slouched through an entire movie because I was worried my head might be obstructing the person behind me, and I didn't want them to think I was one of those inconsiderate people unaware of sight lines in theater-style seating. I've always been hyper-aware of other people's opinions and expectations of me. I used to be in Customer Service, and we subscribed to this motto: Under-Promise, Over-Deliver. Promise less than you can actually do, that way when you accomplish more than your customer's expectations, you will look like a hero. People pleased? Check. In life, any time I can exceed someone's expectations I do a little happy dance inside.

Why am I telling you this? I'm wondering if you, like me, sometimes get stuck on expectations. Maybe it's what others expect of you or even what you expect of yourself. *I need to get to bed earlier. I should have tried harder to find a better price on this mirror. Why didn't I think to invite her to go out with us?*

Then there are times when it's more about expectations you put on other people. That's when it starts to get dicey. I do this with my kids. There's something in me that thinks what my kids happen to be wearing on a given day will be some sort of reflection on me.

When my daughter Kennedy was in kindergarten, she came downstairs before school wearing shorts, a t-shirt, and kelly green socks pulled up to mid-calf. No other green on her anywhere. I said, "Wow... those are some bright socks. Maybe you should find some that match." And before she could reply, my older daughter Quinn said, "Mom, you should just let her wear them. She's in kindergarten. Who cares?"

That's when it hit me. Right. Who cares? If I'm being totally honest, though, the thought that allowed me to let it go was knowing she wouldn't be the weirdest looking one in the class. I mean, it's kindergarten. Those kids are a mess! As long as one other kid was a bigger fashion disaster, then I wouldn't look like the worst parent. Maybe second-to-worst. But not *the* worst. So that's something.

It took my older daughter pointing it out for me to see the unnecessary expectation I was putting on my five-year-old. It takes something specific to "snap us out of it" and see things in a better way. When we set performance standards for ourselves and others, those expectations subtly lead us down a trajectory that gets us way off the mark from reality. And without even realizing it, we've created unhealthy and unnecessary benchmarks for ourselves... and everyone around us.

Spiritually, this happens all the time. We have ideas about how faith should play out in people's lives. What being a Christian should look like. Nothing wrong with that in itself. But when those expectations overshadow God's grace, we've got a problem. And that's where Galatians comes in.

Galatians is a book of undoing. This letter originally from Paul to the church that met in Galatia takes us through a journey of becoming undone. In short, it un-does extra standards we put on ourselves and each other. It leads us to identify how we've let these expectations creep into our daily lives and what we can do about it. Galatians is a layered plea from Paul to live out love unfettered from religious requirements.

But Galatians un-does us in another way, too. As we delve into why our extra-imposed standards are not from God, we come face to face with the unfathomable depths of His grace. We are confronted with a crazy divine economy where our failures cannot outdo God's forgiveness, and our religious practices cannot add to His favor. And when we realize that the formula for security in our relationship with God is ***Jesus + Nothing***, we are unleashed to live fully and freely in that truth.

So consider yourself invited and the journey begun. Yes, even you readers wearing kelly green socks. Let's dig into Galatians and make room for the Holy Spirit to be our undoing.

Chapter 2

Spiritual Bling

In first grade I began attending a program called Sparks at a local church. Part of a larger organization called Awana, Sparks members, or "Sparkies," met weekly to play games, learn the Bible and hear about Jesus. I loved being a Sparkie. I even got my very own vest. It was bright red with a patch bearing the Sparks mascot and our chapter number 442. That was it for the left side of the vest, but the right side? That's where things got interesting.

The right side of the Sparks vest was reserved for all the bling that a diligent Sparkie could earn. There were patches, crowns, and jewels. That's right... jewels! We would spend part of each meeting memorizing Bible verses. I liked this part. As a six-year-old, I could already recite all the names of the books of the Bible, so these bit verses were no match for my mad memorization skills. I could memorize anything. I'd spend the afternoon leading up to the meeting cramming Bible verses into my head like a Jesus junkie on a binge.

Then, the moment of truth. I'd hand my book over to Miss Jackie, spew out the Bible-based words—book, chapter, and verse included—and watch as she penned her official leader signature into my book, confirming my success. Then I was on to the next page of verses. And the next. And the next. Finally, several signatures later, the moment of truth arrived. The jewels!

I watched as Miss Jackie meticulously glued a small plastic gem to a crown-shaped pin. I held out my school-girl hands, eyes widening at the thought that I had earned a single bedazzled crown. And so it began. The years went by. Two more as a Spark, then four in Awana. I amassed bars, patches, pins, dangly metal icons, trophies, a plaque and, of course, those beloved jewels.

My vest was bursting with bling, and my head was bursting with the feeling of approval. Life was good.

Years later, when I began studying Galatians, I learned about an ancient group of Jesus-followers in conflict. The trouble stemmed from disagreement about how to live out their faith. Some of those who had been raised in a Jewish tradition believed their religious practices, rituals, and celebrations were a required part of a Christ-following faith: keeping the Sabbath, circumcision, and observing certain festivals. Others, including those who didn't have a Jewish background, believed the traditions were no longer necessary. The result was a "look how much better I am at following Jesus" kind of comparison-driven division in this struggling Galatian church.

When I picture these early followers, I can't help but remember my award-laden vest. My jewel-earning years were such a valuable faith experience, and about 80% of the Bible verses I know by heart are from those Awana days. But years after I outgrew the weekly meetings, my desire to amass spiritual bling never waned. I performed. I excelled. I strived to create a shiny faith exterior that shouted, "I'm approved!" All the while failing to realize the jewels are not only unnecessary, but have the power to make me forget the incredible depth of God's grace.

That's what began to happen in the Galatian church.

To set the groundwork for what's ahead, think for a few minutes about your own spiritual journey. What practices have become part of your expression of faith?

How might these practices have the potential to diminish your experience of God's grace in your life?

Read these verses, then list what you know to be true of God's grace.

> *We believe it is through the grace of our Lord Jesus that we are saved...* (Acts 15:11).
> *This righteousness is given through faith in Jesus Christ to all who believe. There is no difference between Jew and Gentile, for all have sinned and fall short of the glory of God, and all are justified freely by his grace through the redemption that came by Christ Jesus* (Romans 3:22-24).
> *For sin shall no longer be your master, because you are not under the law, but under grace* (Romans 6:14).
> *And if by grace, then it cannot be based on works; if it were, grace would no longer be grace* (Romans 11:6).
> *For it is by grace you have been saved, through faith—and this is not from yourselves, it is the gift of God—not by works, so that no one can boast* (Ephesians 2:8-9).

Grace is...

Think of grace as your vest, a vest that's everything you need to have a relationship with God. But inevitably, you begin to decorate your vest. It's all good things like going to church and helping the poor. It's studying the Bible and going on a mission trip. It's praying for others and celebrating with them when prayers are answered. All good things.

But over time you begin to notice other people's vests. Some well decorated like yours. Others, not so much. Then suddenly it happens: you begin to believe that you might be a little better at this whole faith thing than someone else. That maybe God might even be a little extra proud of you. Possibly even impressed.

And so, you begin to bling out your vest in earnest. But here's the thing about decorating the vest: it's often a sideways attempt at approval. How are you motivated by approval (whether by God or by others) in the way you express your faith?

What does your spiritual bling look like?

Paul wrote to the Galatians to remind them that Christ alone made their faith complete. Extra rules, practices, and good deeds did not change their standing in God's family. The more honest we are about our own tendencies toward spiritual bling and sought-after approval, the more we will hear the heart behind the book of Galatians. So, let the un-decorating begin!

Chapter 3

From One Blinged-Out Believer to Another

Once upon a time in the land of Gelea, a young warrior named Edrie was endowed with the sacred duty to protect and preserve the hallowed lands north of Promise Prairie. With resolve in her eyes, she set out toward the lands, all the while recalling her training—the battle strategies, the disciplined maneuvers she had mastered over time.

As she hiked along the back trail of the prairie, her medals clanked against one another, and her honor ribbons caught the wind every few steps. She crossed to the rugged sacred lands and began her ascent, and with every step, one thing was sure: She was made for this.

Edrie set up the boundaries, honed her skills, strengthened her reflexes, and taught the travelers who entered the sacred grounds the practices and rituals required to remain in the land.

Most of her time was spent at Crescent Lake, for it was the heart of all the lands her people occupied. From these waters came every river, creek, and rapid, yet no water flowed into it. Its life source came from within itself. The Lake had been there before anything, with one exception—The Divine, who had placed it there for them. She often thought of the stories of The Divine—and a renewed sense of purpose rose up in her until this most beloved and beautiful place became Edrie's obsession.

Years went by, and Edrie's name rose to the ranks of the greatest protectors of the land. She had banished those who were unworthy, who dared touch even a fingertip in The Lake. Only those with discipline matching her own were allowed near its borders, and even then, rigid restrictions had been put in place.

Visitors proved their worth by flashing the pass they had earned through the rigor of a disciplined life. Edrie could spot a counterfeit pass at barely a glance and enforced strict punishment for the frauds. Fewer and fewer inhabitants made it to The Lake, but that was just fine with Edrie. It was sacred, after all. If the waters became polluted, their whole world would crumble. Over time, as Edrie performed her duties, there was a greater and greater distance between The Lake and the people who called it theirs.

Early one evening, Edrie scouted the serene perimeter of Crescent Lake, as was her daily practice. Before her skilled reflexes could react, a blinding flash pushed her back onto the dirt path. She couldn't move. She could barely breathe. Fear like she had never known sat like a rock in her gut. Then she heard the voice.

"Edrie, why are you keeping them out?"

"Who is it?"

The voice rumbled, "I am The Divine. You say you serve Me."

"Everything I do is for You," she whispered, trying to control the uncharacteristic screech in her voice.

"This is not My way. The land, the lake, everything here is for My people. You have mistakenly believed that you are the gatekeeper, but I am the gatekeeper, and I opened the gate long ago."

A moment later, the quiet returned. Edrie was alone again. All was as it had been before. And yet, everything was different.

She ran back, her feet beating the ground as fast as her heart was racing. With each step her treasured medals came loose. One by one they thudded to the ground. As the words of The Divine sank deep into her soul and a rainbow of honor ribbons sailed to the ground in her wake, she felt a growing freedom she had never known before.

Edrie began tearing down regulations she had posted along the trail. She worked feverishly to remove any trace of exclusion. She sent her messengers throughout the night, and by sunrise the next morning, every inhabitant of Gelea knew that Crescent Lake—the sacred place birthed by the hand of The Divine—was open to all. Passes were given freely. Not one was turned away. And welcoming loudest from the top of the ridge, the booming voice of a warrior resounded to the edges of the land.

Twenty-ish years after Jesus' resurrection, Paul wrote a letter to Jesus-followers in a region called Galatia. He had always been a passionate man, and that earnest passion bleeds through each sentence of his writing. His main message in this letter was that the grace of God through Jesus is so complete that nothing we do (or don't do) will cause it to lose its power.

Coming from Paul, this is a profound message. He studied the Law since he was a boy and rigorously followed it. He was a master "do-er." His spiritual vest had so much bling on it that people around him had to wear sunglasses. (But not the kind we have today. That would be ridiculous. They wore the kind they had back then. Back in the ancient Middle East. You know … those ones.)

His vest out-shone, out-ranked, and out-sparkled his friends' vests like the Hope Diamond on display next to a cubic zirconia necklace from the county fair. This man got what it meant to "earn it"!

Paul came onto the religious scene as this new movement of Jesus-followers was getting underway. They preached that Jesus fulfilled the requirements of the Law for us. That forgiveness through Jesus was all one needed to be made right with God. That earning salvation through following the rules didn't work.

Paul wasn't buying any of it.

Embrace the Undoing

So, he straightened his vest, spit-shined his bling, and went on a murderous spree.

Read Acts 9:1-22. This is the biblical account of Paul's (previously named Saul) transition from Jesus-hater to Jesus-follower. If you've read this passage before, consider reading it slowly aloud. Pay attention to anything that stands out to you in a new way.

Imagine being Paul. Create a journal entry as if you were Paul during the story you just read.

Notice what aspects of Paul's journey or perspective are similar to your own (either past or present). When have you believed you were right, and God revealed Himself in a way that changed your perspective?

I imagine during those three days of nothing—no sight, no food, no drink—Paul was re-framing everything he'd ever known, now in light of Jesus. There would have been a sense of loss at first. All the late nights studying the Torah (the Jewish religious Law) when he could have been partying with his friends—like that time they TP'd the Synagogue or decorated the Rabbi's yard with pink plastic flamingos. The early morning prayers. The fasting. The singleness. The constant race toward a glorious, heavenly finish promised by a God that he thought he knew. *What was it all for?*

In Galatians 1:14, Paul describes himself: "I was advancing in Judaism beyond many my own age among my people and was extremely zealous for the traditions of my fathers."

Paul was on a trajectory to be the best vest-bedazzler of all time! He was just hitting his stride, discovering that his mark on the world would be to keep out anyone who did not meet the prescribed holy standards. He was a trailblazer of hard-earned righteousness and had the bling to prove it. But at the end of the three-day darkness, Ananias touched Paul and a never before feeling came over this disillusioned Pharisee.

Freedom.

He became a believer in the only One who can make us right with God. The One who reconciles our relationship with God by being perfect for us so that we don't have to try to be. Paul began to preach the message of Jesus. All his accomplishments and "good-boy-isms" were of no consequence because forgiveness was now the starting point. And forgiveness translates into acceptance, and full acceptance is where freedom is born.

It was this understanding that enabled Paul to write Galatians, entreating his readers to live fully and freely with unshakable confidence in the complete work of Christ. I am moved and challenged by this particular book of the Bible because the more I embrace freedom in Christ, the more I am released from the compulsion to impress God. The more I believe that His work on the cross and His walk from the grave are everything any of us needs, the more I am compelled to see men and women around me as fellow recipients of grace, not as my competition or subject of comparison. I stop comparing my vest to those around me. In fact, I begin to forget about the vest altogether.

I speak for myself—and I think I can speak for Paul, too—that we have much in common with Edrie in the land of Gelea. What about you? Take some time to think about these questions and pay attention to what comes to mind. Use them as prompts and answer as many or as few as you'd like.

- What spiritual "accomplishments" in your life might be misdirecting you away from Jesus instead of toward Him?
- What requirements have you put on others when it comes to faith?
- What is your "Crescent Lake"?
- What is Jesus saying to you about forgiveness, acceptance, and freedom?

Chapter 4

The Galatians and Me

Knowing Paul's spiritual journey before he penned Galatians reveals the deeper layers of his letter. As we move together through Galatians, we can fully appreciate Paul's vehement emphasis on grace alone, in light of his former life as a spiritual over-achiever. Knowing *who* said something often strengthens the impact of *what* was said. Understanding *to whom* something was said matters too.

I'll admit that putting myself in the shoes—sandals—of ancient Galatian believers feels like a stretch, to say the least. What could I possibly have in common with someone who lived two millennia ago on the other side of the globe? She kept water in a cistern. I get it cold from the door of my fridge. She wove her own fabric. I once colored my leg with a Sharpie because my black tights had a hole that I didn't know how to fix. She gave birth without the assistance of drugs. I...wait...so did I. But to be fair, it was an accident. I accidentally gave birth without drugs. Turns out that second babies arrive faster than the anesthesiologist does.

My point: I feel worlds apart from Paul's audience.

But maybe not so much.

The church* in Galatia was experiencing intense conflict over how to live out their faith. The church was comprised of two groups—Jews and Gentiles—who had begun following Jesus. Like any of us, along with their budding faith came baggage from their

Embrace the Undoing

past. Specifically, some of the believers from a Jewish background thought the practices and traditions they grew up with needed to continue in their new faith. And not just their faith, but everyone's faith—including the Gentile believers. The fancy term for these people is *Judaizers*.

Read Galatians 4:8-11, 16-20. In verse 17, Paul is referring to the Judaizers.

8 Formerly, when you did not know God, you were slaves to those who by nature are not gods. 9 But now that you know God—or rather are known by God—how is it that you are turning back to those weak and miserable forces? Do you wish to be enslaved by them all over again? 10 You are observing special days and months and seasons and years! 11 I fear for you, that somehow I have wasted my efforts on you...

16 Have I now become your enemy by telling you the truth? 17 Those people are zealous to win you over, but for no good. What they want is to alienate you from us, so that you may have zeal for them. 18 It is fine to be zealous, provided the purpose is good, and to be so always, not just when I am with you. 19 My dear children, for whom I am again in the pains of childbirth until Christ is formed in you, 20 how I wish I could be with you now and change my tone, because I am perplexed about you!

In light of what you know about Paul's story and what you know about the conflict in Galatia, why do you think Paul was so harsh?

Paul reprimands them for "observing special days and months and seasons and years." He's referencing specific practices the Jewish Law required. It's part of an issue, an example. One piece of a larger problem.

Like when I complain that a holiday wreath shows up at the mall on October 15th. It's my in-passing commentary meant to be a larger whining narrative that everyone is forgetting about Thanksgiving! It's one bit of a larger problem, including Christmas-themed coffee cups in November, "Jingle Bells" background music in a commercial for GAP's fall line, and mid-summer explosions of red and green at my local craft store.

I get it, crafters, you have to start your projects early, but c'mon! You're ruining the back-to-school vibe we are meant to embrace come August.

Small example of epitomizing a larger problem. That's what Paul is doing here. Later, we'll explore his treatment of the Law in this letter (trust me, his commentary goes far beyond this one example). But for now, let's focus on the people.

Picture it. A community of Jesus-followers who are divided in their understanding of how to actually do the Jesus following. One group adheres to a set of outward practices as the mark of the truly faithful. For them, it was the Day of Atonement and New Moons and Passover and Sabbath—rites and rituals that set a high standard for the "really good Christians."

I've never experienced Yom Kipper (Day of Atonement) or Rosh Hodesh (New Moon Festival), but I'm quite familiar with subscribing to a certain set of standards as the mark of "really good Christians." For me, it's practices like going to church, joining a mission team, donating to a charity, reading my Bible, and praying before eating. All good behaviors, for sure.

But like the Galatians, I've been known to muddy the waters between exterior practices and my inner experience of grace. Put plainly, I am the Galatians...I just hide it a little better, and Paul didn't write me a letter about it. (But...as it turns out...he did.)

Consider what external practices might be on your "really good Christian" list.

There's one more layer worth exploring. It's one thing to have a mental list to track our good Christian points. That alone is a big problem, for sure. (The good news is that Galatians helps us overcome that problem.) But besides the list-making, there's a nasty little tendency in us humans that sneaks into this problem, making it even more complicated. That tendency is judgment.

See, if I believe a good Christian does/says/practices X, and I do/say/practice X, but I see that you (fellow Christian) don't do/say/practice X, then I determine that you are not a good Christian. As a math equation it would go like this:

$$\text{Good Christian} = X$$
$$I = X$$
$$\text{You} \neq X$$
$$\text{You} \neq \text{Good Christian}$$

And because our self-centeredness brings everything back to us, there is one more result from our equation:

$$I > \text{You}$$

I conclude that I am a better Christian than you. Judgment. Reflect on how your "good Christian" list affects your view of others.

For Paul's readers, the judgment played out in drastic ways. Their unity was compromised. They began to implode, and the aftermath wasn't pretty.

Reflect on Paul's comments and what they say about the Galatians. How might these verses be speaking to you today?

If you bite and devour each other, watch out or you may be destroyed by each other (Galatians 5:15).

Let us not become conceited, provoking and envying one another (Galatians 5:26).

---

* The church in Galatia refers to all the believers in that entire region. It was most likely several small church communities, not one "church" like we might picture a local church today.

Chapter 5

The Law and Jesus

We happily tacked the hand-crafted "Chore Wheel" onto the corkboard that hung between the tiny kitchen and the even tinier breakfast nook. My three roommates and I had creatively solved the dilemma surrounding the upkeep of the two-bedroom apartment we shared near our college campus. The chore wheel consisted of two pieces of construction paper held together by a brassy brad.

"The chores are divided into four groups, so each of us are responsible for the chores aligned with our name," Karin explained. She was the organized one of the bunch.

Tara chimed in, "I'll vacuum and dust. I can do that fast. I've got two games this week and a paper due."

"I'll take toilets. I want a spot in the garage." Sunny confirmed. The landlord had assigned two parking places per unit in the underground garage. So in the weekly chore rotation, two of us would have the gift of easy-access parking, while the other two had to scramble, fight, and claw for a street space. Garage spots went with the more traumatic chores—bathroom and kitchen duties—because no one who has faced the hair-laden bathroom vanity shared by four college girls has the energy left to search for a parking spot.

Week by week, we faithfully rotated the wheel, and our foursome tackled the housecleaning, avoiding typical roommate arguments about whose turn it was to take out the trash or clean the fridge. But then midterms were upon us, and lab projects, and sorority events and before we knew it, finals. Tara got a boyfriend and was barely home. Sunny had grad-school applications due and hardly left her desk. The trash overflowed, and dust bunnies came for an extended visit. But after each wave of chore-related-failures, we rotated the construction paper circle, buckled up, and started over.

The Chore Wheel reigned victorious, keeping us in check and announcing who was failing.

Fast-forward 25 years.

I share a large open workspace with four of my co-workers. We work at a church built on a 100-year-old dairy farm, and we created office space from remodeled farmhand homes and outbuildings. Our particular "office" has a kitchen area, a living room set-up, and a smattering of tables we use for desks.

While this might sound cushy and fun, what it really is, when you get down to it, is an abundance of surfaces for a lot of used coffee cups and old Post-it notes to be left lying around by unidentified culprits. To add to the chaos, three of the five of us are musicians. Do you know how many guitars one musician needs to own? If you think the answer is one, you'd be wrong. It's more than one. It's often more than two. In a moment of industriousness, one musician hung guitar hooks on the walls. Luckily, for those hooks, they are not required to hold anything very often. They just look out over the room and see the guitars lying on the couch or leaning up against the bar. I feel bad for the hooks. They have one job, you know?

Something had to be done. So we made a Chore Wheel.

Instead of each of us having different jobs each week, one of us is responsible for all the cleaning the whole week. Then we are off the hook (the proverbial hook, not the guitar hook) for four more weeks while the rest of the team takes their turns. So far, the number of chore rotations we have accomplished successfully is zero.

Teresa works in several departments, so she's only there for part of the day.

Jake starts strong on Monday, and it's downhill after that.

Derek gets to the end of his week every time and says, "Wait...was it my week this week? Why didn't you guys tell me?" *We did, Derek. We did.*

I'm only in the office three days a week, so my jobs go undone more than half the work week. When I do clean, I mumble a passive-aggressive commentary on how dirty the sink got, even though Derek cleaned it the week before. But he didn't, see?

Katie does her chores and does everyone else's when they forget. I keep telling her to stop covering for them because "how else will they learn?" That's the naggy mom coming out in me. I like to think it's endearing, but that's not what my co-workers call it.

In summary, Chore Wheel 2.0 is failing. Or, more accurately, we are failing.

And the Chore Wheel silently judges us as it looks over the chaotic room.

Rule-keeping gives us a sense of accomplishment. We check off our lists and obey the rules, and a smug satisfaction settles over us. Until, that is, we miss one. We break an important rule and the list shifts from pats on the back to guilt-ridden fails. Paul writes this in Galatians 2:19—

"For through the law I died to the law so that I might live for God."

Through the law I died to the law? *Huh?*

He's saying, in a roundabout way, that the list of religious requirements was the very thing that brought him to God. Paul realized that the Law was impossible to keep. No matter what level of piety he achieved through sheer striving, it would never be perfect. And a less-than-perfect performance of Law-keeping was a failed performance. Until Christ, the spiritual conversation wasn't "How well did we keep the Law this week?" It was, "How badly did we blow it?" Paul's efforts to be good fell short, showing him that his final destination in the Land of Law-keeping was death.

Christ revealed the full picture of salvation. The rules were never meant to save us. They were meant to show us how ineffective our own striving is when it comes to salvation. Paul realized this when he encountered Christ. The very list of rules that he lived by led him to Christ, because Paul understood that salvation is a gift given by a perfect Savior, not an achievement we can accomplish on our own.

The Living Bible translates verse 19 this way:

For it was through reading the Scripture that I came to realize that I could never find God's favor by trying—and failing— to obey the laws. I came to realize that acceptance with God comes by believing in Christ.

I envy Paul. Intimately knowing the Law like he did made it easier to know how to *not* live under it once he relied on Christ. For us, the demarcation between moral performance and surrender to what Christ already performed is often tough to separate.

What are the performance-driven ways you try to find God's favor?

Read verse 19 in The Message. Read it a few times, maybe out loud. Pay attention to what stands out to you. How does this connect to your own story? What do you sense God might be saying to you in this?

What actually took place is this: I tried keeping rules and working my head off to please God, and it didn't work. So I quit being a "law man" so that I could be God's man.

The Disney movie "Tangled" starts with the voice of Eugene, the unconventional fairytale prince, saying, "This is the story of how I died."

The love story between Rapunzel and Eugene unfolds with classic twists and turns, including villains, chases, misfits, betrayals... and death. (Spoiler Alert) And it is, in fact, Eugene that dies. But Disney magic is real and death is not the end. Instead, it's a necessary climax that leads to the life these animated heroes were meant to live.

We, too, must experience a death in order to live the life God has for us. Galatians teaches us that only when we undergo the death of our performance-driven, good-kid striving, acceptance-seeking ways, can we live the life God offers.

The life God offers is one of freedom. But it might not be the thing you first think of as freedom. We tend to picture freedom as the ability to do whatever we want, however and whenever we want. Free living means living without restrictions.

But freedom through Christ is something entirely different. Deeper. It is the answer to a core need in every single one of us. We have an inherent drive that compels us to get this need met in whatever way we can. For many of us, it plays out in striving to be better, do more, work harder. For others who have run into dead ends too many times, while the need is still there, the effort to get it met wanes because nothing seems to be working.

Interestingly, both paths—the constant striver and the disillusioned worker—fail to resolve the deep need.

At our core, we need to be accepted.

Acceptance is what we long for. Period.

And in that deep need, Jesus is our answer. In Christ, we are 100% accepted. The work of Jesus on the cross and in the resurrection was/is the conduit of God's acceptance. Get that. Our full acceptance by God rests solely on what He did for us. And in that, my friends, is where our freedom resides. This kind of freedom isn't about no restrictions. This freedom is the relaxed, confident assurance that we are known and accepted—that it's an already-done gift, not a reward we have to earn.

When you believe that God's love and acceptance of you cannot be undone by how good or how bad you are, you are free from the compulsion to perform. At all.

The Message Bible conveys our passage this way:

> *Christ's life showed me how and enabled me to do it. I identified myself completely with him. Indeed, I have been crucified with Christ. My ego is no longer central.* **It is no longer important that I appear righteous before you or have your good opinion, and I am no longer driven to impress God.** *Christ lives in me. The life you see me living is not 'mine,' but it is lived by faith in the Son of God, who loved me and gave himself for me* (Bold mine).

What stands out to you as you read this passage? Rewrite this concept in your own words.

In light of what you've been thinking about so far, how would you describe freedom?

For Paul, religious requirements revealed his own ineptitude and brought his striving to an end. There, he met Christ and discovered what it was to live for God. Through faith in Jesus' sacrifice, Paul was set free. And this brings us to verse 21 where everything comes back to grace. He writes, "I do not set aside the grace of God, for if righteousness could be gained through the law, Christ died for nothing!"

Personally, as I've matured in my faith, I've noticed I am not so "black and white" in my theology. More and more, I embrace the weird tension of the gray. It's where pat answers go to die, and nearly clear answers hold hands with about a dozen more unanswered questions. The gray place feels like the right place to be because I'm desperate to hear and follow Jesus. He knows the path and I can trust Him.

I used to think that Jesus leads me out of the gray place. But I'm beginning to realize that often that's right where He wants to be with me.

Grace is this one-of-a-kind bridge between the black-and-white and the gray place. On the gray side, I'm constantly surprised by grace. How it meets me when I'm disappointed with myself. When it whispers a prompt to see the problem from someone else's perspective. The way it doesn't keep score. In the gray place, grace is simultaneously a familiar friend and a new acquaintance.

But in the black-and-white sphere, grace sits immovable as the unchanging, impenetrable act of God's love and acceptance of me. And that's all it is. And that's everything. No matter what happens between God and me in this relationship we have, grace is never not enough. To whatever extent we get that is the extent to which we will experience freedom. I believe this is what Paul means when he says that it all comes back to the grace given through Christ.

Again, The Message communicates this truth in verse 21 in such a helpful way:

Is it not clear to you that to go back to that old rule-keeping, peer-pleasing religion would be an abandonment of everything personal and free in my relationship with God? I refuse to do that, to repudiate God's grace. If a living relationship with God could come by rule-keeping, then Christ died unnecessarily.

What is "personal and free" in your relationship with God?

Reflect on how you might sense God inviting you to more freedom in your life with Him.

How do you see the connection between freedom, acceptance, and grace?

Chapter 6

The Law and the Spirit

My friend's grandma was Catholic, and every room was adorned with at least one picture of Jesus on the cross. I wasn't used to this. It freaked me out. Especially the one in the bathroom. *Was that really necessary?*

I preferred the empty cross. I mean, Jesus isn't on the cross anymore, right? That's the whole point. Resurrection. Victory over death. Empty grave. All that. I felt like Jesus still on the cross was comparable to pausing a movie halfway through and leaving the awkward freeze frame on your TV. (And, in the case of my friend's grandma, putting that TV in every room.)

But as I ponder Galatians, I wonder if I am a little too quickly skipping ahead to the grand finale of Jesus' work—resurrection. It's not that I forget about the crucifixion. It's more that it almost always pairs with the back-to-life part. But Jesus' death is not only where we must start but, on some level, where we must stay, too.

Read the beginning of Galatians 3 below.

1 You foolish Galatians! Who has bewitched you? Before your very eyes Jesus Christ was clearly portrayed as crucified. 2 I would like to learn just one thing from you: Did you receive the Spirit by the works of the law, or by believing what you heard? 3 Are you so foolish? After beginning by means of the Spirit, are you now trying to finish by means of the flesh? 4 Have you experienced so much in vain—if it really was in vain? 5 So again I ask, does God give you his Spirit and work miracles among you by the works of the law, or by your believing what you heard?

Write down initial observations from this passage:

When Paul was with the Galatians in person, years before writing this letter to them, he preached about the crucifixion. He painted a picture so clear, so real, that the people had a visceral response to it. They believed what they heard and experienced the Spirit's work in them.

I began the year at a new school a few blocks from the house where my mom and I lived. Faith had been non-existent in my childhood so far, so I had no idea what I was getting into as part of Mrs. Nelson's first-grade class at the local Christian school.

"Good morning, children," her shaky old lady voice rang out from the front of the room. "Find the desk with your name on it and have a seat."

There were 40 of us. Yes, 40. This was long before elementary class sizes were limited. We were wall-to-wall six-year-olds up against Mrs. Nelson and her trusty aide, Mrs. Kabfleisch. Before the first week was over, I learned a phrase I had never heard before. The teacher uttered it faithfully four times a day—first thing in the morning, before recess, before lunch, and before dismissal.

She would wait until 80 eyes were on her and 40 mouths were closed, then would launch into her pre-prayer saying: "Every head bowed and every eye closed." Then she'd wait. Then she'd pray. That phrase, her curly gray hair, and her knee-length dresses were the main things I remember about Mrs. Nelson, except for one more thing. She was the first one to teach me about Jesus.

In the early months of first grade, I learned about a man named Jesus and His twelve friends, how they were in boats a lot, healing sick people, and telling stories that were kind of hard to understand (both for me and the people back then). By October, Mrs. Nelson told us about the terrible way He died, but that He didn't stay dead.

"Jesus died for each one of us because He loved us so much."

OK, I'm tracking. Sounds good.

She continued, "And you can choose to accept His love and forgiveness."

I want love and forgiveness.

"All you have to do is ask Jesus into your heart."

Wait… huh? What are you talking about, Mrs. Nelson?"

I did not know how to do what Mrs. Nelson was talking about, but I knew—as much as my six-year-old mind could—that I wanted what she was describing. I believed what she said. Now all I had to do was figure out this "Jesus in my heart" business.

Later that week, as the other 39 students lined up for the post-recess drinking fountain gulp, I made my way over to Mrs. Nelson. I pulled her down to my level and whispered, "I want to ask Jesus in my heart." Later that day, just the two of us in the classroom, we talked and prayed together as I expressed my belief in what Jesus did for me on the cross.

It was a real response to Jesus from a girl who believed what He had done for her. It was my first encounter with Jesus crucified. I remember that day of first grade more than any other day the whole year.

Take some time to reflect on your earliest thoughts about the crucifixion (whether many years ago or more recently).

While reflecting on Jesus' death is often difficult, it's a significant practice for those who want to be free from vest-decorating. Speaking to this type of intentional remembering, The IVP New Testament Commentary says, "We need a renewed vision of Christ crucified if we are to gain freedom from illusions of perfection through law observance, for such a vision is a vivid reminder that the cross, not human achievement, is the basis of God's blessing."[1]

What does having a "renewed vision of Christ crucified" mean to you?

Freedom from perfection is intimately tied to Jesus' death for us. His death is what finalized God's acceptance of us. It was done in Jesus... the key word being "done." In the "doneness," we who believe are not only set free from performing but are gifted with the Holy Spirit. This passage in Galatians reminds us that the freeing work was done for us, and through belief alone, the Spirit continues to work in us.

The idea of the Spirit as an unearned gift was a radical departure from traditional Jewish belief. A well-known second-century Jewish leader, Rabbi Phineas ben Jair, writes this about receiving the Holy Spirit: "Heedfulness leads to cleanliness, and cleanliness leads to purity, and purity leads to separatism, and separatism leads to holiness, and holiness leads to humility, and humility leads to shunning of sin, and shunning of sin leads to saintliness, and saintliness leads to the Holy Spirit."[2]

---

1 "Initial Reception of the Spirit (Galatians 3:1-2)." *The IVP New Testament Commentary Series*, by D. Stuart Briscoe et al., InterVarsity Press, 1990.
2 "Miracles by the Spirit (Galatians 3:4-5)." *The IVP New Testament Commentary Series*, by D. Stuart Briscoe et al., InterVarsity Press, 1990.

Phew! I'm worn out from all those steps to the Holy Spirit! My Fitbit would be congratulating me at that point. My soul, however, would be exhausted. But this is not what we see in the experience of the Galatian Christians. Instead, the Spirit began working *when they believed*. Again, this shouts freedom: "You who believe can rest in the work of both the Savior and the Spirit. The requirements have already been met. You are not being graded. Your failure is irrelevant."

Re-read Galatians 3:5. Think about your life over the past weeks or months. What might have been the work of the Spirit in you (whether or not you recognized it as such at the time)? Spend a few minutes thanking the Spirit for the work done in and for you.

The Message puts verse 5 this way: "Does the God who lavishly provides you with His own presence, His Holy Spirit, working things in your lives you could never do for yourselves, does He do these things because of your strenuous moral striving or because you trust Him to do them in you?" Reflect on the tension in your life between "strenuous moral striving" and trusting God to work in you.

Paul is about to take the Galatians back in time to reveal that faith, not moral-code-keeping, has been the catalyst for a life with God from the beginning. Before we join him on that excursion, spend a few minutes in quiet, listening for anything else the Spirit might have for you here.

Chapter 7

Quotable Quotes (Part 1)

Paul writes this in Galatians 3:6-9:

6 So also Abraham "believed God, and it was credited to him as righteousness." 7 Understand, then, that those who have faith are children of Abraham. 8 Scripture foresaw that God would justify the Gentiles by faith, and announced the gospel in advance to Abraham: "All nations will be blessed through you." 9 So those who rely on faith are blessed along with Abraham, the man of faith.

I wish I were one of those people with an arsenal of memorized quotes I could casually insert into everyday conversation. Or, better yet, excerpts from poetry. Now that's classy! The closest I come is when I hear a memorable line—let's be honest, usually a funny line—and quickly memorize it in hopes I can someday plug it into a conversation and join the ranks of the quote-spewers.

I'm still waiting for this to happen, but here are a few currently stashed in my collection:

"I like to use big words to make myself sound more photosynthesis." (From the cover of a journal on a whole table of ridiculous titles in a quaint bookstore in Oregon.)

This was from the mouth of Winnie-the-Pooh: "People say that nothing is impossible, but I do nothing every day."

Embrace the Undoing

One more. Morgan Freeman said this on "Inside the Actors Studio" with James Lipton. It's not funny, but it stuck with me. He was talking about acting (because duh... that's what they always talk about on that show). He said, "Acting is not creative; it's giving the Creator access." I heard the line, I didn't read it. So I can't say for sure that Creator was capitalized in Mr. Freeman's mind, but that's how it works for me. I love that line and have remembered it since first hearing it over 20 years ago. I have yet to subtly slip it into conversation.

Humorous, creative, and pithy quotes get remembered. They stick. Important, trajectory-changing ones do, too. Moving further into Galatians chapter 3, we discover Paul had quite the collection of ancient quotes. Lines with spiritual significance hidden in their simplicity. I imagine him recalling memorized chunks of the Torah that told the story of Abraham.

Abraham was a key character in Israel's story. In fact, until Jesus, he was *the* key character. The father. The patriarch. The one who was first given the promise from God recorded in Genesis 12:1-3:

1 The Lord had said to Abram, "Go from your country, your people and your father's household to the land I will show you. 2 I will make you into a great nation, and I will bless you; I will make your name great, and you will be a blessing. 3 I will bless those who bless you, and whoever curses you I will curse; and all peoples on earth will be blessed through you."

Notice the use of "I" and "you" in the passage. Reflect on what God says He will do. Imagine you are Abraham. Write what you would be feeling in these moments.

Abraham and God's relationship started off with this incredible promise of all that God would do. In response to the promise,

"Abraham went" (Genesis 12:4) to the land where God sent him. He spent the next several years in wild adventures that included a parting-of-ways moment with his nephew, a stealthy reconnaissance mission involving said nephew, and an awkward love triangle with an Egyptian king (Genesis 13, 14, and 20).

And through all this, the promise sat unfulfilled in Abraham's gut. Then Abraham had another encounter with God.

Read Genesis 15:1-6:

1 After this, the word of the Lord came to Abram in a vision: "Do not be afraid, Abram. I am your shield, your very great reward." 2 But Abram said, "Sovereign Lord, what can you give me since I remain childless and the one who will inherit my estate is Eliezer of Damascus?" 3 And Abram said, "You have given me no children; so a servant in my household will be my heir." 4 Then the word of the Lord came to him: "This man will not be your heir, but a son who is your own flesh and blood will be your heir." 5 He took him outside and said, "Look up at the sky and count the stars—if indeed you can count them." Then he said to him, "So shall your offspring be." 6 Abram believed the Lord, and he credited it to him as righteousness.

I'm intrigued by the conversation that took place a few millennia ago. I translate it like this:

GOD
No worries, Abraham. You've still got me. I'll protect you.

ABRAHAM
Hey, God. That's great and all. I mean, I get that you're a big God and everything, but there was this one part of the promise that I feel like you might have forgotten.

GOD

Hmmm. Let's see. Lead you to this land? Check. Make you into a great nation? I'm on it. Livestock, check. Servants and soldiers, check. Grow your family...

ABRAHAM

There is it! That's the bit you missed.

GOD

Listen, I...

ABRAHAM

It's been years and still zero children! What the heck? Sure I've got this growing household, but I can feel my bones rattling inside me and I'm one uneven sidewalk away from a broken hip! Have you seen these dark spots on my hands? Those weren't there a few years ago. The doctor looked me right in the eyes and said that they have a medical name but they just call them "old man spots." Old man spots! And don't get me started on how big my ears have gotten. Are you aware they never stop growing? What were you thinking on that?

GOD

Are you done?

ABRAHAM

I'm saying I'm old.

GOD

Yeah. I got that.

ABRAHAM

When I die—and let's be honest, that'll be sooner than later—all my stuff won't even stay in my family... because

I have no family! Freakin' Eliezer will be in charge! That guy is the worst!

                    GOD

Dude. Chill.

Abraham opens his mouth as if he will continue talking, then thinks better of it. With a sigh, he collapses onto the dirt.

                    GOD

Abraham, son, you have so many plans. I have not forgotten. I will do what I promised. Let me show you something.

God invites Abraham to see His promise in the stars.

Read verses 5-6 again. Reflect on the change in Abraham. What do you think caused Abraham's shift toward belief?

Find a time you can go outside at night in the next few days and look up at the stars. How do you notice God's presence? How might God be inviting you to move toward belief in your life?

"Abraham believed the Lord and it was credited to him as righteousness" was a new reality that was cemented into the story of God's people. It matters because even in this earliest glimpse of God's plan for saving humanity, we see the spiritual dynamic that plays out to this very day: God's action coupled with our faith. Paul wrote to the Galatians to bring them back to the centrality of this dynamic: God does. We believe.

There was power in Paul's regurgitation of this verse from Genesis because, for his readers, this quote came with the full recollection of Abraham's journey with God. A journey that started everything. They would have recalled even more of the story than we've explored here, so to grasp the full effect, let's keep going.

The rest of Genesis 15 tells of a strange occurrence. Strange because it involved five animals, three of which were cut in half—so technically, two animals and six half-animals. Five animals. Six halves. Got it? Okay. Weird and about to get weirder. God tells Abraham to lay the halves out in two lines with corresponding animal halves opposite each other. Let's all agree this is unsettling.

As much as I would never want to come across any scenario even slightly resembling this layout, it's important to note that for Abraham, this otherwise disturbing dead animal choreography was deeply meaningful. It was the set-up of a covenant...a sacred promise. In this ancient culture, a covenant was made when two individuals each walked between two rows of animal halves. The essence of the vow was "may the fate of these animals be my fate if I do not keep true to what I have promised." Creepy, yes, but oddly moving.

Abraham lays out the carcasses and then falls into a deep sleep. Genesis 15:17 says, "When the sun had set and darkness had fallen, a smoking firepot with a blazing torch appeared and passed between the pieces." God, personified in fire, passes between the animals, sealing a covenant between Abraham and Him. Let's not miss the significance of only God moving between the animals, not Abraham. A covenant like this was finalized with *both* parties walking down the aisle. Both were responsible to uphold their end of the bargain. Both accepted harsh retribution if their end of the promise was not kept.

But here, only God does it.

Ancient stories are hard to grasp. But if we can get beyond the weirdness of archaic covenant practices, we would see how incredibly grace-filled this act of God was. The promise was all on

God's shoulders. It was as if God said, "If I don't keep my end of the bargain, I will pay. If you, Abraham/Israel/Humanity, do not keep your end of the bargain, I will pay then, too."

And 2,000 years later, He did.

With divine foreshadowing, God took the weight of salvation on Himself and asked us, simply, to believe it.

Spend time reflecting on this story. Imagine you are in the scene with Abraham. What are your thoughts and feelings as you watch what God does?

Is there anything you sense God saying to you personally about your own faith?

Look again at Galatians 3:8:

Scripture foresaw that God would justify the Gentiles by faith, and announced the gospel in advance to Abraham: "All nations will be blessed through you."

Those five words in the middle of the verse are heavy with meaning: "announced the gospel in advance." With the 20/20 vision hindsight offers, Paul reflects on the story of Abraham. He overlays what he knows about a crucified Savior and shows his readers that even in the earliest forming of Israel, the plan for salvation would be accomplished through the work of God and the faith of people.

Chapter 8

Quotable Quotes (Part 2)

"What has God been teaching you lately?"

It's an innocent question, a genuine one from the lips of a friend who really cares about me. She doesn't intend it to launch a mental tornado in my mind, but it does. One second, I'm walking on a nature trail, thankful for our time together that took no less than 17 text messages to coordinate, and the next, I'm in an all-out emotional panic about how to answer her question. The split-second conversation with myself goes like this:

What IS God teaching me?
What should I be learning?
I haven't read my Bible since last week!
I probably missed something important that He wanted me to see.
Am I even growing in my faith?
I'm a pastor, for crying out loud!
What a hypocrite I am.
Well, I better say something!
It had better be good, too.
It can't sound like I haven't been deep into Jesus-learning lately.
I have a reputation to uphold.
Think. Think.

I mumble something from the last sermon I wrote and turn the question back on her. (That's a trick I learned in seminary.) Here's the real question: What is triggering this response in me? When my experience of God goes from internal and personal to external and shared, it becomes layered with expectation. I can't stop it from happening, and I don't handle it well.

It goes back to the vest. While my Sparkies vest is long gone, its bedazzled surface disregarded, the proverbial vest of my "really good Christian" accomplishments is as decorated as ever. I want to keep it that way, and I know just how to do it. I've spent 40 years familiarizing myself with DIY hacks that would impress the most accomplished crafter. Regurgitating Christian buzzwords. Teaching spiritual practices that I may or may not have personally experienced. Strategically sharing in small group settings so as to sound deeply spiritual, but with little actual vulnerability.

But when I'm face to face with a friend who asks how I'm doing spiritually, the spiritual bling is shockingly inadequate. The bigger tragedy is that my vest-maintenance steals my focus away from an intimate experience of grace...which ironically is the only power that can rid me of the vest.

Make a short list of what you do to outwardly appear more spiritual.

In fairness, these pretenses are not all bad. They are not necessarily motivated by deception. Most of us truly long for an experience of God that satisfies us to our very core. The problem is many of us have been taught these outward practices are the primary way you get there. And even if we weren't specifically told this, most of us have a blurry line between the *doing* and the *believing* of life with God.

It's yet another reason we have so much in common with this ancient Galatian community. They were neck-deep in the argument about the role of faith-based practices. Their argument surrounded this question: Are outward spiritual practices a necessary part of authentic faith?

Specifically, does a real Jesus follower need to observe Jewish holidays, abide by food-related restrictions, and submit to the practice of circumcision? Some of the Jewish converts (Jews who had decided to follow Jesus) in Galatia were convinced the answer was "Yes"... or at least "better safe than sorry." While they accepted the good news of Jesus' sacrifice and resurrection, they felt the need to also keep these customs that had been ingrained in Judaism for more than a millennium. These believers, then, pushed their misguided but sincere beliefs onto the Gentile (non-Jewish) believers who were part of the same church.

This disagreement was the very reason Paul was moved to write this letter we are studying. So let's find out what he says in this next chunk of his letter...

There are four Old Testament quotes Paul inserts in Galatians 3:10-14. Most Bible translations have them listed in quotation marks, so they're easy to spot. Let's tackle them one at a time.

QUOTE #1

We find the first quote in verse 10: *"Cursed is everyone who does not continue to do everything written in the book of the law."* This verse is from Deuteronomy 27:26. It's the last sentence in the last chapter of a long section in Deuteronomy (chapters 12-26) that covers all of God's commands for Israel. When Paul pulls this quote from Scripture, he's essentially grabbing the concluding sentence of that which was the basis for every religious practice: the Law.

The essence of this verse is the **doing**. "Do everything." And what happens when "everything" is not done? Cursing is what happens. Not the kind of cursing you let slip when your pinkie toe collides with the table leg, but the kind of cursing that means you are cursed. Harsh. The Israelites' understanding was if these commands were not thoroughly—fully—unwaveringly applied, the inevitable outcome was a curse.

Imagine you are part of the Galatian church, and you make your way to the gathering, anticipating the discussion and teaching that lies ahead. You arrive and are met with a flurry of excitement from your fellow Christians. Someone rushes over, whispering, "A letter has come from Paul. The leaders are just about to read it to everyone."

You absorb every word, eager to expand your new-found faith. The pastor reads this line, "Cursed is everyone who does not continue to do everything written in the book of the law." As you hear the words "cursed" and "do" and "everything" what are some of the conclusions you begin to make?

I imagine for every listener at that gathering a spark of doubt and questioning rose to the surface: *Is there a place for the Law in my religion?* Then immediately: *But I'll never keep all of it! I'm cursed.* In that moment they connected the dots between their failure to keep every command and the pronunciation that they are cursed.

Not Do Everything = Cursed

"Hey, everyone! We're all in big trouble."

Church dismissed.

QUOTE #2

Paul continues. In the very next verse he quotes another Old Testament line: "The righteous will live by faith." Wait. What? I can't keep up with all the back and forth here. Which is it: doing or faith?

Putting yourself in first-century Galatia again, what thoughts are swirling in your head as you juxtapose Quote #1 with Quote #2?

The Old Testament tells the stories of people who were following (trying to follow) God. Their relationship with God, as they saw it, was fully tied to obeying God's commands. Yet, when we look deeper, we're invited to notice that even in their highly rules-oriented religion, faith was the center.

Remember Abraham from earlier in our reading? Paul wisely builds his argument of God's grace as a gift by reminding them that even Abraham—the Patriarch of Judaism—became righteous through faith **before** the Law. But over time…centuries…the people had grown used to placing their faith in the rules/customs/traditions for rightness with God.

Next verse…

QUOTE #3

Continuing his denunciation of the Law, Paul pulls from Leviticus 18:5 to say, "The person who does these things will live by them." There it is again—the "doingness" of religion. The very DNA of the Law is that it demands doing.

Now it's your turn to write this letter to the Galatians. With these three quotes in mind, write your own version of Galatians 3:10-12.

Look back over your personal rewrite of Galatians 3:10-12. This time, read it as words written **to** you. Read it a few times and listen for what God might reveal to you about your own efforts to be right with God.

So far Paul makes his case like this:

Quote 1: The Law is all or nothing. Either you keep every bit of it or you might as well have kept none of it. Failure in the slightest leads to destruction.

Quote 2: Rightness with God comes from faith, not doing. The Law is about the doing. We can't find righteousness through it.

Quote 3: The Law is about the doing. (Did I mention that already?)

This passage is clearly about the Jewish Law. Contemplating it might feel irrelevant (as I'm 99.9% sure you aren't struggling with whether or not it can save you), but I wonder if many of us do rely on outward "spiritual" accomplishments as a way to feel more reconciled to God. Going to church regularly. Maintaining a consistent "quiet time." Not swearing. As we practice this good living, we are tempted to believe these acts affect our standing with God.

It's not too far a leap to infer that if the action-dependent Law led to a curse, our action-oriented efforts might have some negative side effects, too. Not a curse, per se… but maybe sort of…

It's impossible for me to read the word "curse" without my head filling with images of Indiana Jones, Hogwarts, and a tiki necklace from my favorite Brady Bunch episode. I'm fully comfortable with curses existing in the world of books, movies, and TV. In fact, I'm all for it! I know at the end of the story, the curse is overcome. (Even if three Brady episodes are required for the tiki necklace to reach its final demise.)

But real-life curses? No thanks.

QUOTE #4

We find Paul's last Old Testament quote of this section in verse 13. "Cursed is everyone who is hung on a pole." It's another callback from Deuteronomy, just like the first quote. This one's from Deuteronomy 21:23. The original passage is referring to a criminal being put to death for their crimes, dying under a curse so to speak.

Pretend for a minute you are a human thesaurus. Create a list of words and phrases to replace "curse." In other words, a list of curse words. Wait... er... I mean... not a list of curse words but a list of synonyms for *curse*.

Pick one word or phrase from your curse words (I couldn't resist) and fill it in where you see the word "curse(d)" in verses 10 and 13 below:

> *For all who rely on the works of the law are under a _____, as it is written: "_____ is everyone who does not continue to do everything written in the Book of the Law."... Christ redeemed us from the _____ of the law by becoming a _____ for us, for it is written: "_____ is everyone who is hung on a pole.*

Read the passage a few times with different fill-ins from your list. Does one seem to click for you? Is there one that adds a fresh nuance to this passage?

The prophet Isaiah writes:
> *... he poured out his life unto death,*
> *and was numbered with the transgressors.*
> *For he bore the sin of many,*
> *and made intercession for the transgressors* (Isaiah 53:12b).

Embrace the Undoing

What do you understand about this passage in light of Paul's quote from Deuteronomy 21:23?

Take some time to intentionally reflect on what is resonating with you. What is the Holy Spirit inviting you to consider regarding Christ's work on the cross and the curse?

The irony, Paul writes, is while the Law gets in the way of grace, it also points us to it. In using these four quotes, he changes our trajectory toward "spiritual accomplishments" which—it turns out—are futile, toward Christ alone. Our inadequacy to keep the rules is the very thing that points to Jesus. He overruled the rules. Paul comes to this exact conclusion later in the chapter:

So then, the law was like a tutor, assigned to train us and point us to the Anointed, so that we will be acquitted of all wrong and made right by faith (Galatians 3:24, The Voice).

No one wants to believe they are cursed. Many of us don't even want to believe a curse is a real thing! I know I don't. So it's tempting to jump to the end of the story, the happy ending, where Jesus canceled it. The Message Bible poignantly phrases it this way: "He became a curse, and at the same time dissolved the curse" (Galatians 3:14, MSG). I like the last half of the sentence.

But the richness of the last half of the sentence is only fully appreciated in light of the first half, what Christ took on for us. The more clearly we see the trajectory we were on—the one that leads to death—the more we can embrace the fullness of Christ's work. And going one step further, placing extra value on our own rule-keeping diminishes our capacity to grasp the completeness of what Jesus did. Knowing the curse was real, that Christ took it on and dissolved it, and that we are required to do nothing more than believe is about the most freeing realization there is.

So what *has* God been teaching me lately?

How to rest in the freedom that He's not keeping score. And I don't have to either.

Chapter 9

The Thing About Hamilton

In the summer of 2017, I learned more about America's founding fathers than I did all throughout high school. That's not a dig on my history teachers as much as a commentary on my complete lack of interest. That summer coincided with Lin Manuel Miranda's *Hamilton* coming to San Francisco, for which we had four seats with our names on them for a Sunday night in August. My older daughter, 13 at the time, was obsessed with this Broadway smash about Alexander Hamilton told through a mix of musical styles including R&B, hip hop, soul, and pop. She knew every lyric. Every. Lyric. Forty-six songs.

We spent the weeks leading up to the show on a road trip through Oregon, underscored by the *Hamilton* soundtrack. After each song, we'd pause and make our young teenager explain what we'd just heard. What was going on in the story? Who was singing? What was the song saying? She was a reluctant musical tour guide, but I think a small part of her enjoyed schooling her parents and sister on 18th-century duel etiquette, constitutional backstory, and what a "bursar" is.

While I love acting and have done my share of performing, truth be told, I'm not the biggest fan of theater, especially musicals. By the time our *Hamilton*-heavy vacation came to an end, though, I was eagerly anticipating the show. It delivered. In fact, it went beyond my expectations in every way. I was emotionally moved, intellectually stimulated, and artistically inspired.

Experiencing the music with the added visual context made what was already meaningful, powerful. After hearing the music, I had the bones of it. But only when I heard and saw and smelled and felt the story in that far-back red velvet seat did I know it. There was one song in particular that was incredible on the soundtrack, but I didn't fully "get it"—the context, the emotion, the deeper layer—until I saw the full scene.

Broadway soundtracks are one example of limited exposure sustaining us for a while. But eventually, if we're to experience the full story, we have to encounter it live—in person—with all the visuals paired with the music we already know. It's no different than what we've been reading about in Galatians.

The ancient covenant with Abraham (the one we studied earlier in which God promised a blessing) was the soundtrack, the limited exposure. It was a vague picture at best, with the Law being a significant part. Going forward for many, many generations, the picture remained fairly static. Until Jesus. Then the full story was finally revealed, the redemption of humanity through Him. The Law (soundtrack) was merely a placeholder. Only in light of the complete life and work of Christ can we experience the full picture as it was meant to be.

Galatians 3:14 says, "...in order that in Christ Jesus the blessing of Abraham might come to the Gentiles..." (NASB). (This short verse closes out the section where Paul went crazy with Old Testament quotes. Re-read Galatians 3:10-14 as a refresher.) Verse 14 simmers down Galatians' theology into a bite-sized chunk. Granted, one we could chew on for the rest of our lives without consuming it entirely.

Let's do a little chewing here, shall we?

He became a curse for us (vs. 13) in order that through Him Gentiles would have the same blessing God gave Abraham.

Remember, the blessing was about becoming God's people, about God making a way for that to happen. And what Paul's readers knew, but seemed to be forgetting, was that way was Jesus.

Chew on verse 14. What does that blessing look like in the big picture of faith? What about in your life specifically?

In Jesus, the covenant blessing wasn't disregarded; it was enlivened! The Abrahamic Covenant was just the beginning. It was the soundtrack. When it was all they knew, it seemed to be enough. But Jesus was the live show. The full expression of the covenant promise. One aspect of that expression was the inclusion of Gentiles. Redemption was for everyone.

The rest of verse 14 fleshes out more of the blessing: … "so that we would receive the promise of the Spirit through faith" (NASB). How would you describe the three key words in this phrase?

Promise:

Spirit:

Faith:

As you think deeper about these words, what might God want you to know about your potential to live in the redemptive work of Jesus?

Abraham marks the starting point, the "where we've been." Jesus finalizes our position as redeemed people. The Spirit, then, empowers us to perpetually remain in Jesus, embracing His work on our behalf and nurturing our personal faith to live into all that He offers us as those under grace.

After seeing *Hamilton,* I played the soundtrack any time I had the chance. Driving to work. Wiping down sticky countertops. Opening the mail. It was the same soundtrack I had been listening to all along, but now there was one glaring difference: I had seen it! With every song, my memory exploded with a mental re-enactment of the full production. I could visualize the scenes and characters, the body language and facial expression, the costumes and special effects, the choreography, and the set. The music triggered a new experience of the story, again and again.

This is what the Spirit does for every bit of religion that came before Jesus. The Spirit reframes all of it in light of the resurrection. When Paul, an expert in Old-Testament-following, reflects on Israel's backstory, he sees it differently because of Jesus. He longs for his readers to do the same. We could even go so far as to say he re-interprets it and invites them to do so as well. He draws out their Old Testament knowledge through a smattering of ancient quotes and urges them to view all of it with post-resurrection eyes.

We have the same eyes…we have full knowledge of the resurrection. We know the story. When we—like the Galatians—get stuck in the trappings of achievement, performance, accomplishment, striving, and score-keeping, we must depend on the Spirit to lovingly grab our faces and point us to Jesus alone. In that posture, we meet grace.

What trappings distract you from grace?

What in your life might need reframing in light of the resurrecting power of Jesus?

Spend a few more minutes meditating on Galatians 3:14. Ask the Holy Spirit to lead you to a deeper understanding of the blessing God has for you through Jesus.

Chapter 10

Promises, Promises

The biggest problem with our penchant for written messages—text messaging, messages through social media, or even a standard e-mail—is that tone is difficult to convey. Imagine you send a text message asking a co-worker if she wants to join you for lunch on Monday. She replies, "Sure." Nothing wrong with her answer. But don't you wonder about her unheard tone? Was it an enthusiastic "Sure!" or a more resigned "Sure"?

In your mind it morphs into a multiple-choice test question.

Agnes asks Phyllis to lunch on Monday. Phyllis replies, "Sure." What did Phyllis mean?

1. Yes! I can't wait! You're one of my favorite people!
2. Yeah. Why not? I gotta eat.
3. Um...OK...I guess. Is there a reason? I mean, we don't go to lunch much, so I'm wondering if you're going to bring something up with me. Like, are you mad at me or something? Did your other lunch plans fall through? Am I your backup plan? That's sort of offensive, but how will I know if I don't go to lunch? So, yeah, I suppose we could go to lunch. Uhhh...sure...

Tone. It's hard to read.

Embrace the Undoing

By this point in the Galatians' journey, though, we're starting to "get" Paul and have a fairly good sense of his tone. He's definitely passionate. A little defensive sometimes. Angry in places. And it might be my own sarcastic nature, but I find that when I imagine Paul's voice in his writing, it has highly patronizing tone in places.

In my head, I hear him yelling, "You guys, are you seriously not getting this?" Followed by a teenage-worthy eye roll and a disgusted sigh. "YOU GUYS!! C'MON! L-I-S-T-E-N-T-O-W-H-A-T-I-A-M-S-A-Y-I-N-G!"

That might just be me. I'll leave it up to you to form your opinion as we approach these next few verses in Chapter 3. We last left Paul in the middle of building his case for grace like a top-notch attorney.

Recap: He reminds his readers they have experienced the promised Holy Spirit they received by faith. They know the Spirit's presence is a gift they did not earn (Galatians 3:2-5). He has them think again of Abraham and how even the earliest beginnings of Israel's relationship with God were rooted in faith alone (Galatians 3:6). Using their ancient religious texts, he proves the impossible-to-keep Law is what leads to death (Galatians 3:10-13). That the promise hinges on Christ and leads to life (Galatians 3:14).

At this point in the argument, Paul steps away from his laptop and drags himself to the bathroom. Planting his hands on each side of the sink and pressing his weight forward, he looks in the mirror. Eyes bloodshot. Hair going in myriad directions. Stale breath like the stink of a thousand mornings. This essay is really taking its toll on Paul. *Why do I bother?*

With a deep breath, a sigh, and the half minute it takes to re-center, Paul knows. He knows why he bothers. Because it matters. More than matters... it's life itself (this side of heaven anyway). This paradigm shift away from personal performance toward the fully sufficient work of Jesus is everything, affects everything. If he can lift the veil for these Galatians, like his own religious veil was lifted on that road so many years ago, then everything can change for them, too.

So, he tops off his coffee and gets back to work.

I'll take this from a different angle.

> *15 Brothers and sisters, let me give you an example from everyday life. No one can get rid of an official agreement between people. No one can add to it. It can't be changed after it has been made. It is the same with God's covenant agreement. 16 The promises were given to Abraham. They were also given to his seed. Scripture does not say, "and to seeds." That means many people. It says, "and to your seed." That means one person. And that one person is Christ. 17 Here is what I mean. The law came 430 years after the promise. But the law does not get rid of God's covenant and promise. The covenant had already been made by God. So the law does not do away with the promise. 18 The great gift that God has for us does not depend on the law. If it did, it would no longer depend on the promise. But God gave it to Abraham as a free gift through a promise* (Galatians 3:15-18, NiRV).

Spend some time with this passage. What thoughts come to mind as you read? What do you notice? What stands out to you?

Look over what you wrote. Do you have any new insights? Or do you notice themes/realizations/phrasings that have repeatedly come up in your reflections so far? What do you sense God might be saying to you? Take time to listen. Resist the urge to move on in the chapter simply to "get it done." Enjoy the freedom to receive what God has for you.

Paul dots the word *promise* throughout this passage (and in the sections to come). *Promise* is a heavy word. It's full of expectation and anticipation. My younger daughter has a tendency to rewrite history and insert promises that weren't originally part of the story.

"Sorry, kiddo, we're not going to have time to stop at the park."

"But you **promised**," she exclaims in a pitch at least an octave higher than her usual tone.

"No, I didn't."

"Yes, you did!"

These back and forth opposing declarations go on for three more rounds. It's not super clear who the adult is in the banter, but when I look in the rearview mirror and see her young face, I deduce I'm the adult here. I've got to put a stop to this.

"Honey," I say, morphing into my Super Mom alter ego, bestowed with the powers of mustered-up patience and tongue-biting abilities that squash the "I'm the boss" and "Because I said so" replies about to erupt. I continue, "I didn't promise. In fact, you might notice that I hardly ever promise because I've lived long enough to know that 97% of my intentions go undone. I've accepted the lack of control over my schedule, my pacing, and my priorities on any given day. So while I admit to potentially saying 'we might go' or 'we'll try to make it,' I definitely did not promise. Promises are a big deal. I make them as infrequently as possible."

At this point, she has stopped listening. She's back to reading the *Highlights* magazine she found tucked in the car seat back pocket. (I should point out another Super Mom skill is replying with long-winded monologues, during which the kid loses interest and forgets what she wanted from me.)

Promises are a big deal. For both parties. **The promiser is required to be faithful. The promisee is required to have faith.**

It's not hard to find a book of Bible promises or a list of all of God's promises. Verses cataloged in these places offer encouragement, hope, and perspective. Good stuff. But frankly I'm not convinced every one of these verses should have made the cut for the "lists of promises."

Take Psalm 18:3 which I found on a list of Bible promises. It says, "I called to the Lord who is worthy of praise and I have been saved from my enemies." What a powerful testimony! I called on God, I praised Him because He is worthy, and He saved me from my enemies. I am all for this verse. I want this verse to be indicative of my life just like it was of David who penned it.

But is it *really* a promise?

I mean. C'mon. I don't see an actual promise here, do you?

The "list of Bible promises" we can easily Google is chock full of verses like this one. Some lists boast over 5,000 Bible promises, though most of the verses don't contain a promise... or even the word "promise."

Now, if I were you reading this right now I'd wonder, "What is going on here ?"

*This is a bummer. Why is she pointing out there are **fewer** promises in the Bible? I want more, not less! I thought she wanted to encourage me, not pull the promises rug out from under me. What gives?*

Settle down, friend.

Here's my point.

The lack of specific promise language doesn't lessen the significance or meaning of verses we find on Bible promise lists. They still tell the faith stories of those who have gone before us. They still bring light in the midst of darkness and peace in the midst of worry.

The absence of specific "promise" vernacular does not reduce the value of these Bible texts. But this is what it *does* do: it draws our attention to the much shorter collection of references that quite clearly *do* speak of a covenant pledge made by an all-powerful God to us measly humans. I get the sense we should pay attention to those.

> Here are a few of them…
>
> Ephesians 1:13-14 - *And you also were included in Christ when you heard the message of truth, the gospel of your salvation. When you believed, you were marked in him with a seal, the promised Holy Spirit, who is a deposit guaranteeing our inheritance until the redemption of those who are God's possession—to the praise of his glory.*
>
> Hebrews 10:23 - *Let us hold unswervingly to the hope we profess, for he who promised is faithful.*
>
> James 1:12 - *Blessed is the one who perseveres under trial because, having stood the test, that person will receive the crown of life that the Lord has promised to those who love him.*
>
> Ps 119:41-42 - *May your unfailing love come to me, Lord, your salvation, according to your promise; then I can answer anyone who taunts me, for I trust in your word.*
>
> Ps 119:162 - *I rejoice in your promise like one who finds great spoil.*

Sit with these verses a little longer. Circle the word "promise" and pay particular attention to what it conveys in each context. Where can you make connections to your own life? How might God be speaking life into you through these passages?

As for references to the promises that are specific to Galatians, we find Paul writing with a very clear trajectory in mind:

- The promise God made to Abraham was a covenant of reconciled relationships with God.

- That promise was enabled through Jesus who, in turn, promised the Holy Spirit.
- The Holy Spirit breathes life into the promise by securing our reconciliation and empowering us to live reconciled lives.

This theology of promise keeps the onus on God. The burden, if you will, of salvation (life with God) is entirely on Him. It rests in His faithfulness and love. It was put into motion by Him. It was revealed through Christ. It is perpetuated through the Holy Spirit.

The work, the *doing*, is and will always be on God.

Our contribution is believing that His work is enough.

Paul's entire thesis of Galatians is this very concept. He conveys it so strongly, pushing against the believers' tendency to value their own performances as if it adds even an ounce to their standing with God. When we understand what lies beneath Paul's passionate response, we hear his tone a little more clearly. (This is why I suggested we can infer an underlying exacerbation in Paul's writing here.) There is a desperation to convey this all-important message.

So if we are to be listeners and receivers of Paul's message, let's consider what obstacles in our own lives prevent us from fully embracing all God has for us through the fulfilled promise. The Law tripped up the Galatian believers. What's tripping you up?

Essentially, it boils down to how trustworthy we believe God to be. If His original promise placed all the responsibility on Himself, do we really believe He will come through for us? It can be hard to trust we don't have to do anything other than believe. It feels too good to be true.

Have a conversation with God about these questions. Ask for help to overcome the obstacles that lead you to believe you must add to His grace. Thank Him for the sureness of His promise.

Chapter 11

We've Got Attachment Issues

The rag-tag group circled the community table, its marred faded surface dotted with paper cups proudly displaying The Friendly Bean's logo. The group intermittently sipped their steamy caffeine-laden drinks as they listened to one man. He was central, leading the impassioned discussion with wild gestures and an ever-ascending pitch. The other five showed the concentrated strain of their whole-hearted attempt to embrace what was being said.

"Paul, why then was the Law given at all?" The burly man across the table asked.

"Exactly!" A petite woman to his right added. "How does it go from being everything to nothing?"

Paul turned his sharp eyes to the pair, then glanced at the other three around the circle. "It was because of sin ... all of our misguided tendencies and harmful choices. We needed something to guide us until the plan was revealed."

"A temporary solution." This was from a wrinkled woman with a twinkle in her eye.

"A temporary fix ... that we became too attached to," Paul said. "It wasn't 'nothing,' but the Law has run its course."

The first man continued, "You're saying that our Law, which tradition states was given to Moses through angelic beings, is not eternally binding?"

"Like we've discussed, the Law was added to the promise."

"That's true. Over 400 years later," the younger woman added.

"Yes," Paul rushed on, "the Law came *after* the promise. It was secondary. Supplemental. Extra. If angel mediators presented the Law to Moses, that makes my point for me!"

"Because…?" the gruff voice across the table prompted, almost getting it.

"Because God Himself made the covenant with our father Abraham. There was no middle man as in the giving of the Law."

Continuing her thought from a few moments prior, the elderly woman whispered reverently, "The Law isn't—and never was—central to God's plan for our redemption."

"Yes, you're getting it. Christ alone, the fulfillment of the original promise, is the eternal solution."

The fresh-faced kid, looking no more than nineteen, leaned forward, elbows sticking to the table like magnets. "I still don't get why He gave the law at all if it opposes the promise given to Abraham. Was He trying to confuse us?"

"The Law doesn't oppose the—"

"They can't both be eternal." The quiet man seated next to Paul spoke for the first time.

Squeezing the man's shoulder, Paul looked tenderly at him until the man returned the gaze. "Right. It's not both, friend. Only the promise. The promise that made the way for Christ."

Truth dawning on him, the man said, "The Law was never enough. It never could have been."

"Yes." Paul nodded. "It was the placeholder for humanity, essential for a time, but never intended to bestow righteousness. It came *after* the promise and only until Christ."

Understanding dawned in the youngest one. "The ancient rules can't lead us to a right life with God because all they do is reveal our sin."

Paul added, "That's precisely what the Law is for…to make us aware of our inescapable sin."

The young man nodded and said, "The Christ was the only one to escape... and the only one with the power to free us as well."

"And once we grasp that, this promise we have of life through 'the Seed' becomes all the sweeter." With an arthritic hand the old woman reached for her tea as a subtle but knowing grin rose to her lips.

For the first time since they'd gathered a few hours earlier, a thoughtful silence spread over the group. Paul sipped his now-cold black coffee, knowing even he couldn't add to that.

This is what I imagine Paul's conversation would have been like with the Galatians, if instead of arriving in a letter, it had been in person. And if instead of huddled in a church-goer's home, the group sat amidst modern-day coffeehouse logos and those communal tables that seem to be all the rage at said coffeehouses.

To get a sense of Paul's actual written words, read Galatians 3:19-22.

> *19 Why, then, was the law given at all? It was added because of transgressions until the Seed to whom the promise referred had come. The law was given through angels and entrusted to a mediator. 20 A mediator, however, implies more than one party; but God is one. 21 Is the law, therefore, opposed to the promises of God? Absolutely not! For if a law had been given that could impart life, then righteousness would certainly have come by the law. 22 But Scripture has locked up everything under the control of sin, so that what was promised, being given through faith in Jesus Christ, might be given to those who believe.*

In these meaty verses, Paul is adding to his argument that Christ alone reconciles us to God. The Law, he says, was put in place to *show* us our sin... not fix us. It couldn't solve our problem of unrighteousness because its very function was to show how unrighteous we are. These rules, then, were put in place only temporarily—after the promise "until the Seed to whom the promise referred had come."

The era of clinging to the Law was over. It was time for the permanent answer (Christ) instead of the placeholder (Law). One commentary puts it this way: "…the common Jewish perspective of [Paul's] day…emphasized the eternal, immutable nature of the law. But Paul's Christocentric perspective led him to see that Christ (the promised seed), not the law, was the eternal One."[14]

With so much of Paul's dialogue dedicated to dismantling the power of the Law, it can be tempting for us modern-day Christians—who aren't struggling with the role of the Law in our daily lives—to assume there is no application for us here. Especially this section that speaks of angels and mediators and "the Seed." So much Jewish nuance!

Instead, let's explore what the Spirit may have for each of us in these verses. Yes, it's a bit removed in its specific theological context, but could we again align ourselves with these Galatian readers and see if there is more to hear from this text than we might have first thought? Think about it in terms of *attachment*. They were overly attached to the Law. Their striving to meet the standard made them appear righteous in their own eyes, while distracting them from grace-given righteousness that God made available through Jesus. They chose to be attached to the Law instead of the Savior. As for us, might we become overly attached to spiritual benchmarks that distract us in the same way?

While this may feel repetitive, once again list some practices or characteristics you would categorize as essential to the life of a believer.

I'm guessing your list is full of good things... good practices designed to draw us close to God. Ironically, though, accomplishing these ideals has the potential to diminish our connection with God. Consider where and how that might be happening in your own life.

From your personal experience, is there anything on this list you do out of compulsion, keeping up appearances, or the sense that you owe God?

How might that detract from your experience of Christ?

Saint Ignatius of Loyola* was a theologian from the early half of the 1500s. He was a Spanish priest who founded the Catholic order called the Jesuits (or the "Society of Jesus"). Looking at his life prior to the wartime injury that changed his entire spiritual experience, one would never have predicted Ignatius would become a pillar of the Church.

Picture a philandering, appearance-obsessed, worldly man morphing into a prays-for-hours-at-a-time and has-deeply-profound-experiences-of-Jesus kind of guy. He was even jailed for being too passionate about serving and teaching others to do the same. Much later, Ignatius returned to school and then seminary in order to be officially deemed a leader in the Catholic church. He didn't start out as a highly spiritual man, but God used him instrumentally in the Counter Reformation.

My Protestant upbringing left little room for me to be exposed to this spiritual thought leader until much later in life. We did cover

Ignatius in seminary, but in the throes of grad school demands, youth ministry directing, and hoping my then-boyfriend-now-husband would ask me out, my ability to engage in the teachings of this 16th-century monk was limited to regurgitating facts that would get me through my Church Patriarchy class. (*Sorry, Dr. Thompson... I know that's not a stellar testimony. It's me, not you.*)

So, while I'm confident that at some point in my life I could answer test questions about Ignatius' life and theology, it wasn't until many years later I began absorbing the personal implications of Ignatian Spirituality. I learned about him, but I had not experienced him. It's like how you can know a Cronut *exists* but not really *experience* it until the delicious croissant-donut-hybrid-baby touches your very own lips.

Ignatius is my Cronut.

In his writing, he incorporated the language of *attachment*. To what are we spiritually attached? What are we attached to more strongly than we're attached to Christ? As I overlaid this question onto my own life, "attachment" became an important framework for how I viewed my relationship with God. Specifically, the phrases "ordered" and "disordered" attachments provided perspective on my list, the one I have made cataloging all the things good Christians should do... be... become.

Here's a basic rundown of ordered and disordered attachments: If we imagine everything we experience as a gift from God—our opportunities, relationships, personalities, belongings, environments—we can "hold" these gifts in one of two ways. Either we can grip them tightly or hold them loosely.

When we grip them tightly, they tend to become more and more important. Over time, we grow so connected to them—identifying ourselves with them—that our dependence on them becomes greater than our dependence on God. Ignatius calls this "disordered attachment" because that to which we are attached is in the wrong order. God's gifts, instead of God Himself, become our primary attachment.

But when we hold the gifts loosely, meaning we value them as ways we can grow in our love of God and each other, we are able to keep God as our primary attachment. For example, I have an outgoing personality. I can make a stranger laugh in two sentences or less. My personality type makes people feel welcomed and at ease. As a speaker, I'm often told that I'm a "breath of fresh air." Just how I'm wired. My personality, like all of our personalities, is a gift from God. It's part of the uniqueness He has given each of us.

When I view my personality as a gift from God that I can use to engage with others in a way that helps me grow in my love for them and/or my love for God, I am holding this particular gift appropriately loosely, so I can keep holding God appropriately tightly. God is what I'm attached to first. I have an "ordered attachment."

It's important to note that this can change in a hot second. While I might experience ordered attachment one day—hour—minute—it can flip incredibly fast to become a disordered attachment. When that happens, my personality traits become the place I find my worth. The way I feel validated or valued. If I stay on this disordered trajectory, I begin to depend on this gift God's given me more than on God Himself. My personality—meant as a gift to help me love God and others better—becomes a place of pride, judgment, and all sorts of yuck.

This constant pendulum swing from ordered to disordered and back again is yet another special talent we humans keep messing up. But it is also a place where we can know the continual depth of God's grace... again and again. Yay for this grace that stays divinely immovable as I fluctuate from loose to tight gift-holding!

Think about ordered and disordered attachment in light of your "good-Christian-to-do list." Every item on the list has the power to grab your attention and your attachment in a disordered way. For Israel before Christ, it was the entire Law. For the Galatians after Christ, it was select pieces of the Law they couldn't fully let go of.

What is it for you? What are the goals of to do, to be, to strive, to improve, to stop, to continue, to fix... that steal your attachment? Reflect on your well-intended spiritual efforts that have the potential to steal your focus from God.

When these become disordered attachments, how is your ability to experience grace impacted?

Spend time in conversation with God about what is coming to light for you. Either through prayer or journaling, tell God what you are noticing about your attachments, and then listen for what you feel God might be saying to you in response. Engage in a conversation with God in whatever way you feel led.

(I often find it helpful to write out a conversation with God. I write what I want to say to God or ask God. Then I listen for what I think He is saying back to me. Sometimes a verse comes to mind. Sometimes a word. Sometimes He asks a question back to me. I've never been much for journaling, but I find that when I do slow down enough to write, it often enables me to slow down enough to listen.)

---

* For deeper insights about Ignatian Spirituality, I recommend *The Jesuit Guide to (Almost) Anything: A Spirituality for Real Life* by Reverend James Martin, SJ., HarperOne, 2012.

Chapter 12

I'm In!

I rejoiced at finding a parking spot on Main Street's quaint downtown. Jumping out of the car with keys and coffee mug in hand, I herded my youngest out of the backseat and toward the theater door. We were on time for her play rehearsal (miracle). Score one for me. I visualized a big green checkmark on the "Mom is winning" list that ran in my head.

The theater program in which my daughter was enrolled was a few towns over from where we lived. A "few towns over" can make all the difference in status—financial, social, and otherwise. This town was on the upscale side, and I often felt out of place here. I was an imposter... a poser.

With plans for a brisk walk while she was in rehearsal, I wore workout clothes, a hat, and tennies. I bent down for our quick goodbye smooch and she went inside. Then it happened. As I turned from the door toward the sidewalk, I saw *her*... the other mom. In an instant I absorbed the full picture: workout attire (check), grungy hat (check), keys dangling off one finger (check), and a coffee cup in the other hand. A real mug, not a travel tumbler (check and check). Just like me. Just like me! Here before me was a local "in the wild." A native-to-the-fancy-town who looked just like me. My immediate thought: *I'm in! I'm not an outsider anymore. I can definitely hang with this crowd.*

I had arrived. So. Many. Checkmarks. My second miracle of the morning. Crazy how something as insignificant as clothing can birth something as significant as belonging. (Or at least the *feeling* of belonging.)

During the few steps to our respective cars, a bounce appeared in my walk and my confidence ticked a notch higher. But... alas... it was short-lived. A dose of reality crashed into my mental list as I unlocked my dust-crusted Ford. And she gracefully slid into her Mercedes. Nooooooooo! I guess we weren't alike after all.

It all started in pre-school when our teachers gave us worksheets entitled "What Doesn't Belong?" A duck, a cow, and a dog populated three of the four squares. A boot in the fourth. We grabbed our favorite red crayon and slashed through the out-of-place shoe. That's the day we became experts in knowing what's in and what's out.

And eventually... *who's* in and *who's* out.

There we have it. Another similarity between us and the recipients of Paul's letter.

Remember, the conflict among believers in Galatia revolved around the question of "How much of the Law should be part of living out our faith?" Since those in the church arrived at different answers to that question, there was a divide. At its most basic level, it was a who's-in-who's-out divide.

Was there a time in your growing-up years where you felt like you were *in*? Maybe it was making a sports team, getting invited to a birthday party, or winning a spelling bee. What did it feel like to be *in*?

What about today? Think of one or two situations where you are in the "group." It might be something you've worked for like your place on the org chart at work, or it can be as basic as being in the small percentage of people who actually look good in skinny jeans. Groups dot our entire existence ranging from denominations, to looks, to our neighborhood, to social justice activity, to gym memberships, to environmental friendliness, to what grade our kids are in... or even what grades they get. List a couple of your groups.

Belonging and being included checks off a lot of boxes in our psyche. A sense of belonging is a core emotional need for humans. The flip side of *our* belonging, though, is the tendency to categorize others as not belonging.

In Galatians 3:26-29 Paul writes:

26 So in Christ Jesus you are all children of God through faith, 27 for all of you who were baptized into Christ have clothed yourselves with Christ. 28 There is neither Jew nor Gentile, neither slave nor free, nor is there male and female, for you are all one in Christ Jesus. 29 If you belong to Christ, then you are Abraham's seed, and heirs according to the promise.

Read the passage again. This time, circle or highlight unifying words like "all" and "one" and "belong."

These verses push against our ingrained line-drawing, group-making, category-assigning mentality. In his writing, Paul is specifically speaking against the long-held Judaic belief that Israel was in and everyone else was out. Verse 29's declaration that all believers are included as Abraham's "seed" and "heirs" broadened the scope of who is in God's family. Jewish tradition said that Abraham's actual, physical descendants (Jews) were the intended recipients of God's promised blessing. Now, however, Abraham's "seed" is redefined. "United with Christ, believers receive Christ's status as Abraham's offspring."[3] Paul argues that Jesus moved the inclusion line. Belonging to Israel was no longer the parameter. Belonging to Christ was. Through Jesus, now everyone could be *in*.

Imagine you are one of those in the Galatian church who was a Jewish convert (born Jewish, raised Jewish, then chose to be a Christ-follower). Describe the tension you might feel as you read this part of Paul's letter.

This new mindset of Christ alone—not the Law, not circumcision—as the way to God's family was a complete trajectory shift from Jewish tradition. Their preschool worksheets showed three squares filled with Moses, Abraham, and David. The fourth was a Gentile "sinner" who didn't belong.

One commentary writer puts it this way, "In the old set of relationships under the law, Jews were the children of God and Gentiles were sinners. But now Gentile Christians are all sons of God through faith in Christ Jesus. This must have been a shocking declaration for a Jew to hear. In Jewish literature, sons of God was a title of highest honor ... now Gentiles—the rejected, the outsiders, the sinners, those who do not observe the law—are called sons of God."[4]

---

3 "Galatians 3:29." *Jewish Annotated New Testament*, by Amy-Jill Levine, Oxford University Press, 2017.

4 "New Spiritual Relationships in Christ (3:26-27)." *The IVP New Testament Commentary Series*, by D. Stuart Briscoe et al., InterVarsity Press, 1990.

For us to grasp the depth of the dividing lines for Jews, let's explore one more layer that will unlock the deeper meaning of verse 28:

There is neither Jew nor Gentile, neither slave nor free, nor is there male and female, for you are all one in Christ Jesus.

Even within Israel's own community, there was a strong awareness of categories. It was commonplace for a Jewish man to regularly recite this prayer, still found today in Orthodox practice:

Blessed are you, O God,
who has not made me
a gentile, a slave or a woman.

From a Jewish perspective there were clear lines of demarcation like what we see in this prayer. A Jewish man had much to be thankful for, including not being "a gentile, a slave, or a woman," groups that were a few (or many) notches down on the religious hierarchy. With verse 28, Paul superimposes an entirely new reality in Christ. No more categorizing who's in and who's out based on male/female, slave/free, or Jew/Gentile designations. Those groups were based on us. Paul declares instead that we "no longer see each other in our former state" (Galatians 3:28 TPT). We are "all one in Christ Jesus" (Galatians 3:28 NIV). Or as Billy Graham put it, "The ground is level at the foot of the cross."

Think again about the groups or categories you are in. Do your positive feelings of belonging ever feed a negative perspective that you are better, more worthy, more "on-track," more spiritual or more Christian-*ish* than those who are not in the group? In other words, is there any self-righteousness underlying your sense of belonging?

Spend time praying or using the space here to write out a prayer, talking and listening with God about what He's bringing to mind.

Ultimately, this inclusion with Christ is yet another gift God gives us to which we can choose to be attached in an ordered or disordered way. Remember, an ordered attachment is evidenced by us using a gift to love God and others more. No matter how varied our expressions of faith, if grace has been received through Christ, "God's promise to Abraham belongs to you" (Galatians 3:29, NLT) and her and him and them.

So for all the ways we are *in*, let's use that sense of belonging to know and love God better. And let us never allow our own *belonging* to be a catalyst for excluding, judging or looking down on others. Instead, may it spur us on to love others (inside and outside of our categories) well.

Chapter 13

The Unnecessary Three-Legged Race

Think back to when you were a child or teen. Did you ever participate in a three-legged race? It's when you tie one leg to a partner's leg (making three legs... hence the name). Then you see how fast you can run. Typically, you experience one or two falls, a lot of yelling, a possible twisted ankle, and at least one bruise from where the tie dug into your shin or thigh. Running this way is cumbersome, to say the least.

Now, think back to what it felt like to race. Just a straight up, see-who-can-run-the-fastest, race to the finish line. I was never a great runner, but even *I* remember the exhilaration of all-out abandon, limbs pounding against the air, lungs burning, and feet flying. Do you remember that feeling of freedom?

Both of these memories can characterize our spiritual life. Sometimes encumbered and burdened. Sometimes wild and free.

Before reading the next Galatians passage, spend time contemplating what this has looked like for you. How would you describe the following?

My faith feels burdensome when...

Embrace the Undoing

My faith feels unencumbered when...

Keep these thoughts in mind as you read Galatians 4:1-5 and discover what three-legged races have to do with an ancient Roman practice.

> *1 What I am saying is that as long as an heir is underage, he is no different from a slave, although he owns the whole estate. 2 The heir is subject to guardians and trustees until the time set by his father. 3 So also, when we were underage, we were in slavery under the elemental spiritual forces of the world. 4 But when the set time had fully come, God sent his Son, born of a woman, born under the law, 5 to redeem those under the law, that we might receive adoption to sonship.*

In this passage, Paul refers to a common Roman practice that would have been very familiar to his audience. But, as often happens with modern readers like us, the depth of his message is lost until we wrap our minds around the analogy. So, let's take a peek into the life of an ancient Roman son.

> *Hi. My name is Max. Well...Maximus, but I prefer Max. Tomorrow is my 14th birthday and I know it will be the best one yet, because I finally get to be my father's son again! You're probably thinking I ran off, or was disowned or something scandalous. But no. That's just how we do things around here. See, as far back as I can remember, I knew that someday I would be in charge of my whole family. I'm the heir, after all. (I'm not trying to brag, I just want you to know the backstory.) When I was little, my dad introduced me to a man named Claudius. He told me that Claudius was going to take care of me. Train me. Teach me. Essentially, raise me. I was expected to follow his rules down*

to the letter. So that's what I did. At first it was hard. I barely saw my family. They treated me like a slave, not a son. But I knew that this was the way it was supposed to be. Not one day went by where Claudius wasn't with me. He corrected me when I messed up. He reprimanded me when I made the wrong decision. He rewarded me when I got it right. I answered to him in everything. But tomorrow? Tomorrow is different. I turn 14 tomorrow and that's the day my father adopts me to sonship. Tomorrow I go back to my family and live the life I was meant to live.

In Roman families, especially wealthy ones, parents would hand their sons over to a guardian for the bulk of their "growing up" years. It was the guardian's job to train the child and remain in charge until "the time set by the father" (4:2).

Picture yourself as one of those Roman sons. Imagine the time you were under a guardian, and write what you would be feeling or thinking.

What would you be looking forward to when the time came to be brought back into your family? What fears or concerns might you have?

Paul uses this cultural practice as an analogy, paralleling how Christ frees us from being slaves and brings us into God's family. There is a *before* and *after* in the story of the Roman son.

BEFORE:
- The son is no different than a slave (4:1)
- The son is subject to guardians and overseers (4:2)

AFTER:
- The son is "adopted" back into the family
- The son is reinstated as the heir

Spiritually, Paul says, the same thing happens for us. Before Christ, humanity was subject to the Law. But when the time was right, the Father sent Jesus to free humanity and open the door to receive "adoption to sonship."

Going back to the end of the previous chapter in Galatians read 3:23 to 4:7, identify which phrases describe the spiritual **before** and which describe the **after**. Underline one and circle the other (or use colored pencils if you're feeling crafty).

Galatians 3:23-4:7

23 Before the coming of this faith, we were held in custody under the law, locked up until the faith that was to come would be revealed. 24 So the law was our guardian until Christ came that we might be justified by faith. 25 Now that this faith has come, we are no longer under a guardian. 26 So in Christ Jesus you are all children of God through faith, 27 for all of you who were baptized into Christ have clothed yourselves with Christ. 28 There is neither Jew nor Gentile, neither slave nor free, nor is there male and female, for you are all one in Christ Jesus. 29 If you belong to Christ, then you are Abraham's seed, and heirs according to the promise. 1 What I am saying is that as long as an heir is underage, he is no different from a slave, although he owns the whole estate. 2 The heir is subject to guardians and trustees until the time set by his father. 3 So also, when we were underage, we were in slavery under the elemental spiritual forces of the world. 4 But when the set time had fully come, God sent his Son, born of a woman, born under the law, 5 to redeem those under the law, that we might receive adoption to sonship. 6 Because you are his sons, God sent the Spirit of his

Son into our hearts, the Spirit who calls out, "Abba, Father." 7
So you are no longer a slave, but God's child; and since you are
his child, God has made you also an heir.

BEFORE is described as…

AFTER is described as…

Once we understand the implications of this passage on a macro level (think: all of humanity, for all time) we can weave those implications into our faith on a personal level. Starting with the big picture, here's what we know from studying Galatians so far:

- For hundreds of years (or "For thousands of generations") before Christ's work on the cross, God's people lived out their faith by obeying the Law.
- Jesus' death and resurrection fulfilled the requirement of the Law for us and "redeem[ed] those under the law" (4:5). This means that since Jesus conquered death (the ultimate curse of the Law and sin) when we accept His grace we can be freed from the control and the punishment of the Law.
- Those who have received this grace, join God's family. They are now heirs to God's promise of salvation and are freed from the control of the Law.

This is the communal, historical experience of God's people. While this trajectory of **before** and **after** describes God's work for all humans, it also reveals the trajectory for each of us individually. Paul writes about both trajectories at once. He implores the church in Galatia to

Embrace the Undoing

remember the big picture of Christ's redeeming work on the cross. But Paul also challenges them to examine their own lives and realize that they were living the "**before**" life of slavery to the Law instead of the "**after**" life of freedom in Christ (Galatians 3:1-5 and 4:8-11).

Think again about the ways your spiritual life might be characterized by performance and expectations. It's as if we entered a running race, but chose to tie our leg to someone else's because we misunderstood what kind of race we were running. We thought we were running in tandem with rules and requirements, all the while not realizing that these were the very things preventing us from freedom we have in God's grace. Paul teaches us that we are no longer bound to performing a certain way, we are now empowered to live freely as children of God!

What words describe your spiritual life when you are (or have been) motivated by performance, rules, and expectations?

What words describe a life lived in freedom?

Remember Max, our Roman son character? What a homecoming he must have had! Imagine yourself as Max. Picture the scene. Close your eyes and feel what he might have felt. Unleash your imagination. Even if you wouldn't call yourself a creative type, you have a lovely God-given imagination in there somewhere. Write out the scene, paying particular attention to how Max *feels*.

Max used to be described as a slave but now is a son. Not a slave, but a son. Paul implores believers to live not as rule-followers, but loved children. What is God telling you that you are *not*, so you can live into who you *are*?

Maybe you are...
    ... not being graded but forgiven
    ... or not rejected but embraced
    ... or not judged but empowered
    ... or not punished but nurtured

Read through the personal observations and insights you wrote in this chapter. Review your imagined scene too. Choose words or themes from your reflections and create a personal statement about who (or what) you are *not*, and who (or what) you really *are*.

Not _____ but _____

Write your statement out and put it somewhere where you will see it regularly.

When it's all said and done, here's the truth: grace shows us that Jesus ran the race for us. No additional running is necessary to be a child of God. No hobbling across the finish line tied to a cumbersome list of rules. But there is something about living in freedom that compels us to run just because we can. So, let's un-tie ourselves from rules and requirements that have already been satisfied in Christ and run freely to our place in God's family as loved, fully accepted children of God.

Chapter 14

For Goodness' Sake

In the very first paragraph of this book, I admitted to having some people-pleasing tendencies. It's nothing out of the ordinary. Most people have this problem, right? (*She says to her therapist.*) My assumption is that everyone cares deeply about what their mail carrier thinks of them. I've been told repeatedly, however, this is not the case. It's not "normal" or "healthy."

Fine. I suppose I can concede that my people-pleasing-problem (the PPP) is not an issue everybody has. But, the underlying fears that drive the PPP? We can all relate to those. Fear of rejection and fear of failure. Can we all agree just reading those two words feels like a double gut punch? *Ooooof.* Twice.

Fear of rejection says *if I don't do everything I can to make this person happy, they might leave or stop caring for me.* Fear of failure says *if I make a mistake, I will disappoint people and/or be punished.* Your own rejection fears and failure fears might not play out in a PPP like mine, but have you considered how those two fears affect your perspective on what God thinks of you?

Re-read the descriptions of what fear of rejection says and what fear of failure says. How do you relate to these perspectives?

Embrace the Undoing

To what extent do they characterize your relationship with God?

When I think about the people in ancient Galatia—who are beginning to feel like old friends by now—I wonder how aware they were of these twin fears of failure and rejection. As we learn their story and piece together their struggle, aren't we more and more convinced that the rejection/failure fears so present today were similarly present then, too? With that in mind, let's approach the next section of Galatians 4, where we will discover that a compulsion to please others—or even God—can rob us of Christ's life in us.

Galatians 4:8-20 reads like a dramatic monologue from a Hollywood blockbuster. If possible, stand and read it out loud with Oscar-worthy passion. Try it with one of the "everyday language" versions like The Message (included here), The Voice, or The Passion Translation. (WARNING: If you are in a public setting, please DO NOT do this. I repeat DO NOT stand and read out loud. No one will appreciate it. You will not receive an Oscar. You likely will be asked to leave. SECOND WARNING: If you are in a public setting, please DO NOT try to adjust this exercise by simply mouthing the words and gesturing wildly without any sound. Same goes: no one will appreciate it. You will not receive an Oscar. You *definitely* will be asked to leave.)

OK, on the count of three go... or don't go... depending on where you are right now.

One. Two. Three!

8-11 Earlier, before you knew God personally, you were enslaved to so-called gods that had nothing of the divine about them. But now that you know the real God—or rather since

God knows you—how can you possibly subject yourselves again to those paper tigers? For that is exactly what you do when you are intimidated into scrupulously observing all the traditions, taboos, and superstitions associated with special days and seasons and years. I am afraid that all my hard work among you has gone up in a puff of smoke!

12-13 My dear friends, what I would really like you to do is try to put yourselves in my shoes to the same extent that I, when I was with you, put myself in yours. You were very sensitive and kind then. You did not come down on me personally. You were well aware that the reason I ended up preaching to you was that I was physically broken, and so, prevented from continuing my journey, I was forced to stop with you. That is how I came to preach to you.

14-16 And don't you remember that even though taking in a sick guest was most troublesome for you, you chose to treat me as well as you would have treated an angel of God—as well as you would have treated Jesus himself if he had visited you? What has happened to the satisfaction you felt at that time? There were some of you then who, if possible, would have given your very eyes to me—that is how deeply you cared! And now have I suddenly become your enemy simply by telling you the truth? I can't believe it.

17 Those heretical teachers go to great lengths to flatter you, but their motives are rotten. They want to shut you out of the free world of God's grace so that you will always depend on them for approval and direction, making them feel important.

18-20 It is a good thing to be ardent in doing good, but not just when I am in your presence. Can't you continue the same concern for both my person and my message when I am away from you that you had when I was with you? Do you know how I feel right now, and will feel until Christ's life becomes visible in your lives? Like a mother in the pain of childbirth. Oh, I keep wishing that I was with you. Then I wouldn't be reduced to this blunt, letter-writing language out of sheer frustration.

And the drama-queen award goes to... Paul! To be fair, he's being dramatic for a valiant reason. I hope your personal rendition included fist-shaking and spit-flying. Seems apropos for its author. He recalls the generous, loving, and kind acceptance of him (and of grace), then blasts them for sabotaging this beautiful trajectory. He warns that "heretical teachers... want to shut [them] out of the free world of God's grace..." (verse 17).

I'm moved by Eugene Peterson's paraphrase in The Message version of verse 17, where he describes the church's misplaced devotion to those trying to teach that grace alone was not sufficient. Paul ascribes a motive to these false teachers: "so that you will always depend on them for approval and direction."

And... we are back to the need for acceptance and approval, fear of rejection and failure. The teachers who were bad-mouthing Paul had created a codependent relationship with the Galatian believers. Like the snobby popular girl in every teen movie from the 80s and 90s, the false teachers set a sky-high standard that must be reached to be good enough. Like the wanna-be awkward nerd character of those same movies, the church-goers wanted to meet the standard to finally feel the rush of approval.

Paul steps in to put a stop to it.

Way back in Galatians 2, he set the stage by saying:

My ego is no longer central. It is no longer important that I appear righteous before you or have your good opinion, and I am no longer driven to impress God. Christ lives in me (Galatians 2:20, MSG).

Wow! It's one thing to declare you don't depend on others' opinion of you, but to take it a step further to "I am no longer driven to impress God"? That's just too far!

Or... is it?

Do you try to impress God? What do you think of the idea of not needing to impress God? Reflect on what God might have for you here.

How does grace offer freedom from the fears of rejection and failure? What might that mean for you on a personal level in your relationship with God?

The more we lay aside the standard-striving and vest-decorating (which have become second nature to us), the more Christ is formed in us. Or as Peterson phrases it in The Message, "Christ's life becomes visible" in our lives (4:19). And that's the good stuff. The actual, Jesus-in-us good stuff.

It's goodness minus our futile attempts to earn extra credit points with God. It's simply the goodness that is possible as we live in grace. Authentic goodness that can be unleashed when we express the freedom that grace brings. Goodness from Jesus in us, not from the compulsion to look shiny on the outside. Goodness that is a result—or a fruit—of the Holy Spirit.

Paul encourages their desire to do good but reminds them to check their motives. He is wise to notice that when we are driven by performance, our goodness can stem from a desire to impress God or others. The original Greek in Galatians 4:18 conveys:

It's always good to burn with zeal in things that are excellent, beautiful, or commendable and not just when someone you want to impress is watching (Galatians 4:18, Andrea paraphrase).

Embrace the Undoing

Who do you try to impress with your goodness? What is your motive?

On the flip side, is there anyone in your life who truly brings out good in you? (The freedom-driven goodness that isn't borne out of the compulsion to impress.) How do they do this?

What are the characteristics of someone who brings this kind of freedom—not requirements—to your life? Do you do that for anyone else? Could you?

Challenge: In the next few days, take time to specifically thank someone who bolsters goodness in you without making it about pleasing or impressing them.

The more we embrace the truth of Jesus' complete work on our behalf, the more readily we can release our preoccupation with dazzling other people with our good deeds. The hidden motives come undone because they are no longer necessary. Then there is room for goodness to shine through us solely because of Christ in us.

The Voice translation sums this up beautifully in 2 Corinthians 3:3 (another of Paul's letters):

You are the living letter of the Anointed One, the Liberating King, nurtured by us and inscribed, not with ink, but with the

Spirit of the living God—a letter too passionate to be chiseled onto stone tablets, but emblazoned upon the human heart.

Stay with this verse for a bit. What is it saying to you in light of what God has been revealing to you so far?

Chapter 15

Identity Crisis

Do you remember learning to write your name? My last name was short, but it included a few extra letters for no reason at all. *Wright.* A six-letter name where only three of the letters make sounds. As a kid, I memorized all the letters—even the extras—and I knew I was a "Wright."

I, of course, also knew I was an "Andrea." I enjoyed writing the "e" as a capital. E. Only the "e." I did, however, have trouble remembering how many horizontal lines were supposed to be there. So I would draw the vertical line, then add no less than nine horizontal lines. Just to be safe. My "E" looked like the head of a rake.

In high school I spent considerable time pondering the all-important decision of what my official signature would look like. This mattered. It would be on future checks and even the back of a credit card someday. It was much more important than my measly chemistry homework, so my practice time was parsed out accordingly. I'm happy to report that by then I had moved past the rake-E. I fiddled with signature options, added as many swirls and scoops as the letters would allow, and inserted my middle initial. If Michael J. Fox could do it...

At 25, Wright became Coli, and I exchanged a last name with too many silent letters with one where people try to add extra letters.

"What's the last name?"

"Coli."

Embrace the Undoing

"C-O-L-E-Y?"
"No. C-O-L-I."
"Two Ls?"
"Nope. Just the one. C-O-L-I."
The pen hesitates. They still don't get it. Why only four letters?
I say, "It's like E. coli without the e."

They chuckle over the connection to a dreaded infection and are magically released from their inability to grasp such a letter-vacant last name. (Unfortunately, my explanation causes them to pronounce it "COLE-eye" which is wrong, it's "CO-lee," but I suppose I can only ask for so much from the hostess at Applebee's.)

Names are fascinating. The mention of a name calls to mind the whole essence of someone. What they look like, how you know them, how they make you feel. Reading these names, who comes to mind? Cindy. Kristen. George. Jodi. Chris. Emily.

See? Just a simple name prompts you to recall who someone is to you.

Andrea is who I am. I grow and transform. Still Andrea. Wallow in a week-long funk. Still Andrea. Make a mistake. Still. Be my awesome-est self. Same. How I behave does not change the name I've been given. It's my identifier.

In our conversation so far, we've amassed several identifiers for those who belong to Christ. We are "sons," not slaves, righteous through Jesus, promise-receivers, freedom-enjoyers, faith-bringers, and covenant-recipients.

Reflect on one of these phrases (or make up a new one) that holds particular value for you as you've been journeying through Galatians. Why does it feel significant? What mindset or pattern has this truth corrected for you? How has it enabled you to more fully receive God's grace in your daily life?

Galatians 4:21-31 presents an allegory of two women and two children. The picture is meant to solidify our belief that grace—not our efforts toward being good—is our identifier. Grace tells us who we are.

Whether we are the best version of ourselves or the worst, our "of-God-ness" does not change. When our identity is in His faithfulness and relies on His unchanging grace, our behavior cannot change it. He is our name.

How readily we align ourselves with who God empowers us to be, certainly does change our experience of Him (more to come on that in the next chapter of Galatians). But before we can live that out in a spiritually healthy way, we must first ground ourselves in grace alone.

The allegorical story goes like this.

Many years ago there was a woman named Sarah whose deepest sadness came from not having a child. God promised that a great nation would be born to her husband Abraham, but years later, they were still childless. Sarah believed her dream of having a child was long dead. She grew old, giving up all hope of a family of her own. She wondered, though, if there was another way and offered her servant Hagar to Abraham to sleep with and have a child that way.

Hagar was young and healthy, and it wasn't long before she had a son. But a few years later, so did Sarah. She held the long-awaited Isaac in her arms and knew without a doubt she was looking at a miracle. After a while, Sarah resented Hagar and wished her own son Isaac was Abraham's only child. One day she saw Ishmael, Hagar's son, picking on Isaac. Sarah's anger burned within her. She threw Hagar and Ishmael out of their family and wished he had never been born.

The two sons (the child of flesh and the child of promise) represent two ways we try to find God. Ishmael, the son of the servant woman, represents human striving. The great religious effort to make our way to God. This way is marked by enslavement to the Law: the rules that can only bring condemnation. The impossible-to-keep moral code. The minding of ritual and out-of-reach perfection.

Isaac, the son born to Sarah through the miraculous act of God, personifies the grace-filled way to God through Jesus. This second-born son, the result of God's divine promise, represents the true way to God. This way requires our faith and God's work.

This is what we know to be true: If we have found God by way of grace, we are true "sons" whose identity rests in Jesus. But just like Ishmael picked on Isaac, it's as if the Law has been picking on grace.

The Law shouted to the struggling Galatian believers, "I was here first; you can't simply disregard me!" *But here's the thing, Law, you weren't here first. God initiated a covenant promise based on faith alone. You, Law, were just the placeholder, remember? Stop demanding that we find our identity in how well we follow you, because nothing can change who we really are: children of God through grace.*

Brainstorm a short list of attributes to describe the "child of promise" and the "child of flesh" from the story.

Thinking specifically about their identities, how might Isaac and Ishmael have viewed themselves?

When it comes to you finding God, which son most closely depicts your own spiritual history? How so?

Spend a few minutes listening and reflecting on what God's message to you might be in this story.

The most mind-blowing part of all of this? No matter which son you *feel* like, in Christ, you are a child of promise. Your identity is secured and unchangeable because of Christ's complete work. This is what Paul's been emphasizing again and again throughout Galatians. In this particular passage, he does so by way of an analogy assigned to characters with whom the Jewish people are very familiar: Sarah and Hagar. "Paul's purpose for his allegorical interpretation of Genesis 21 is to identify the Galatian Christians as the children of freedom and to instruct them to resist those who would lead them into slavery under the law."[5]

Read Genesis 16:1-16 and 21:1-21 for the original Old Testament account of these two sons. Once you have gained context from the Genesis passage, read Galatians 4:21-31.

Paul culminates by saying, "And you, dear brothers and sisters, are children of the promise, just like Isaac" (Galatians 4:28, NLT). This sentiment echoes an earlier verse that says, "If you belong to Christ, then you are Abraham's seed, and heirs according to the promise" (Galatians 3:28).

---

5 "Galatians 4:21-31." *New Testament Commentary Series*, by D. A. Carson, Inter-Varsity Press, 2007.

Embrace the Undoing

It's not arrogant or presumptuous to claim this identity in Christ. It is, in fact, quite the opposite. Embracing the promise of salvation God originally gave Abraham as a promise we receive today through Christ requires the humble admission that our own effort is insufficient. That our standing as a child of God is truly a gift of faith.

Within that context, fully accepted because of Jesus, we can confidently live out the freedom that comes when we are no longer compelled to be good enough. To bling out the vest.

Our identity is settled because the work has already been done.

Regardless of your history,
Nevermind your tendency.
Forget about legitimacy.
Christ is your identity.

As you let those words settle on you, use the space below to write out Galatians 5:1. Read it through several times. Consider writing it again somewhere where you will see it throughout the next few days. Regardless of the identifier we were given at birth, freedom is our generous inheritance as children of promise.

Chapter 16

Those Stubborn Trinkets

I'm enamored with the book of Galatians. It's thought to be one of the earliest (some theologians believe, *the* earliest) of the New Testament letters, written only twenty-ish years after the time of Jesus. This chronology explains the bare-bones, no-nonsense approach to a life of faith. I'm drawn to the exaggerated black-and-whiteness of the doctrine. Paul's arrow-like focus on Jesus-plus-nothing comforts me.

What I could do without is all the male body parts references.

Circumcision this. Circumcision that. Circumcision here. Circumcision there.

Is this really necessary?

For the Israelites, circumcision was the quintessential mark of the children of God. Personally, I'm baffled as to why the mark wasn't a simple tattoo or a piercing of some sort. Much easier to stomach. Certainly less embarrassing. Israel's mark could have been a punch card or a club card like the one I flash at the door of Costco. "God-co"? *No, that's weird.* But a code word could have worked. I'd go so far as to say even a lanyard with a special "God" logo would have done the trick. Just thinking outside the box here. Anything but circumcision. Anything but *that*.

Sadly, my suggestions are a few millennia too late. But in reading Paul's treatment of the topic in Galatians, at least I can rest easy that he groups this practice in with the Law-keeping standards that are no longer required. In Christ, the Law has been cut off (pun intended). This delicate topic is unavoidable in Paul's letter, so we might as well get comfortable with the text.

Read Galatians 5:2-6, marking each mention of circumcision.

> *2 Mark my words, I Paul, tell you that if you let yourself be circumcised, Christ will be of no value to you at all. 3 Again I declare to every man who lets himself be circumcised that he is obligated to obey the whole law. 4 You who are trying to be justified by the law have been alienated from Christ; you have fallen away from grace. 5 For through the Spirit we eagerly await by faith the righteousness for which we hope. 6 For in Christ Jesus neither circumcision nor uncircumcision has any value. The only thing that counts is faith expressing itself through love.*

In this passage, what statements does Paul make about circumcision?

Imagine what was going on in the minds of the Jewish Christians as they read Paul's words. If circumcision had always been the mark of the children of God, what are the implications of Paul's words?

Remember the vest? The spiritual vest—much like my decades-old Sparkies uniform—holds the decorated bedazzlement of accomplishments and earnings. Some of us have been adhering bling to it longer than we haven't been. My hope for you in this journey through Galatians is that one by one you have removed the ornaments. You've stripped the vest down to simply the hole-poked fabric.

Or almost.

You may find a handful of those long-displayed charms are rusted stuck. You've tugged. You've twisted. They won't budge. You're not sure they'll ever come loose.

These hangers-on are the long-standing marks of what we believe set apart a Christian: faithfully attending church, standing against things "of the world," trying to live righteously, being "above reproach," or calling out sin. The list is customizable... unique to each of us.

For Paul's original readers, the mark was circumcision. God's true children had this in common. But Jesus changed all that. Remember Galatians 3:26-29?

> *26 So in Christ Jesus you are all children of God through faith, 27 for all of you who were baptized into Christ have clothed yourselves with Christ. 28 There is neither Jew nor Gentile, neither slave nor free, nor is there male and female, for you are all one in Christ Jesus. 29 If you belong to Christ, then you are Abraham's seed, and heirs according to the promise.*

Do you really believe that faith in Christ is enough to be fully accepted by God even if you don't do anything else?

Be encouraged, friend! You have a beautiful, unique story of faith that is unfolding as you and God write your story together. The yes-or-no question of "Do you really believe that faith in Christ is enough to be fully accepted by God?" is certainly worthy of more than a simple yes or no.

Embrace the Undoing

I have found myself answering that question in different ways over the years. Sometimes it's a "Yes…but…" Other times a "No…but…" My trajectory, though, is leading me to a "Yes" without the "but." It's often too hard to accept. Or is it too easy?

I share this to embolden you to continue wrestling with your answer. The Jesus we see in the Bible is more than willing to patiently walk alongside you, engaging in the dialogue that surrounds this question. In many ways, I believe it's the very most important question to consider.

Here's the problem: If we believe Jesus alone is everything we need to be "in" and we recognize the extra requirements we've put on ourselves and others are, in fact, *extra*, what do we do when the extras still have power over us? When they seem to demand our compliance? How do we disengage with what we have labeled as good Christian attributes? Or should we?

Galatians 5:4-6 can be broken down like this:

NIV	Andrea Paraphrase
You who are trying to be justified by the law have been alienated from Christ.	Our adherence to the "good Christian rules" have separated us from Jesus.
You have fallen away from grace.	It also separates us from grace.
For through the Spirit we eagerly await by faith the righteousness for which we hope.	Total righteousness is something that we look forward to as a future reality and only comes by faith.
For in Christ Jesus, neither circumcision nor uncircumcision has any value.	Following the "good Christian rules" counts for nothing.
The only thing that counts is faith expressing itself through love.	What has value is that which is compelled by faith and love.

This passage makes it clear that when we follow the "good Christian rules" as a way to try and be a "good Christian," it does nothing but distance us from Christ and grace. The becoming we long for—the image of Christ—comes as we wait with faith for Christ to do His work in us. And along the way, our good deeds and Christian-*ish* standards have no worth. Truth be known, the only real value is found in goodness compelled by love.

If we aim for outward marks of Christianity out of fear or self-promotion or appearance or advantage, they remain as rusty, gaudy decorations on our vest. And as we've already said, they won't come off no matter how hard we pull. So, how do we remove these counterfeit marks? Answer: we don't.

Love does.

Reflect more on Galatians 5:4-6. What are you still holding on to that has yet to be motivated by love versus performance?

Ask God to show you how to let love undecorate the rest of your vest. If needed, use the space provided to write out your prayer.

We are now in the right headspace and heart-space to receive the remainder of Paul's letter. We, like his original readers, must totally divest ourselves of practices motivated by performance, striving or achieving. Acknowledging their emptiness is the only way to embrace the complete work of grace through Jesus.

With that truth as our framework, we are empowered to live out God's grace in us. Outwardly, our actions may look similar to before. But in reality, everything has changed. Goodness, kindness, sacrifice, discipline…all these things…are now born out of love and are a testament to living in grace, not adding to it. Each time our "deeds" are compelled by love, they are simply evidence of God's life in us. Not more trinkets to adorn our vests.

The rest of Galatians speaks to how we nurture that new reality in our daily lives.

CHAPTER 17

The Alternate Route

I'm addicted to my driving directions app. Addicted might be a strong word. Dependent. Yes, dependent for sure. If my driving directions app paid taxes, it could claim me as a dependent. Our relationship started out casually. Heading to a new destination, I would enter the address and hope for the best. But I've grown to have a visceral need to be told where to drive.

What lane should I be in?
Is there an object on the road ahead?
How many nanoseconds until the exit?

Last week I was using my favorite app while my mom was in the car with me. I wanted to show her that this app was very accommodating. She prefers surface-street-driving, so I simply tapped the "avoid freeways" box and typed in our destination. *Viola! See, Mom, you too can become ~~addicted to~~ dependent on this app.*

I forgot to uncheck the box.

The next evening, heading to a speaking engagement, I robotically entered my destination and followed mindlessly. I'd been to this town before but had never gone this way.

The freeway must be really jammed! Not to worry, though ... my app found this obscure side road that will get me there.

My car flew over the curve and rise of the road. The cows and horses trod lazily among wildflowers and an old windmill. The early evening sun hit the rolling green hills as they swallowed the curvy road up ahead.

I smiled, thinking of the headache-inducing standstill freeway traffic. *Not my problem! Thank goodness for my app.*

At the 6-mile mark, I remembered the still-checked "avoid freeways" setting.

Oh.

Immediately there was a flutter in my stomach. I gripped the wheel tighter, but this move was complicated by the sudden clammy sweat dripping from my hands. The hairpin turns were unforgiving, and the road shrank to dangerously narrow. Chunky black clouds rolled in and a vulture appeared out of nowhere. My wheels bumped over an already-dead something. A dot in the rearview mirror grew into a tailgating pickup, horn shouting, "Hey, newbie, get off my road!"

I persevered on this unwanted adventure. Frenzied and panicked, I arrived at my speaking engagement. Thirty-eight minutes late.

There's more than one way to get from point A to point B. Had I to do it over again, I would have chosen a different route. My backroads journey reminds me that the way we choose to go (even if that way was chosen for us by our app settings) deeply affects our experience along the way.

Through grace, Jesus offers us the way of freedom. The way that enables us to love generously because we are unencumbered by piety. In the way of freedom, we receive God's love as a gift, fully convinced it cannot be earned, and we express God's love genuinely, unfettered by the "be a good Christian" checklist.

The way of freedom, by its very definition though, is one we constantly choose to follow or not follow. Grace encompasses us so deeply that freedom itself comes with the freedom to choose to *not* live freely.

My brain shorts out when I try to comprehend the depth of that truth. Genuine freedom means we are free to not live freely! *How often have I chosen the way of bondage instead?*

Though "bondage" might sound heavy-handed, living according to anything other than love is bondage to something—either to myself or to the rules I've blindly accepted.

Consider the last 24 hours. Identify a moment where you acted in a self-serving way or a rule-following way that was not marked by love. Reflect on what your deeper thoughts and feelings were in that moment. Talk to God about this and listen for His response.

Now, identify a moment where you acted out of love. Reflect on what was going on inside you in that decision. In what way did it feel life-giving to your soul? Invite God into your reflection and celebrate this moment together.

Galatians 5:13-14 says:

13 You, my brothers and sisters, were called to be free. But do not use your freedom to indulge the flesh; rather, serve one another humbly in love. 14 For the entire law is fulfilled in keeping this one command: "Love your neighbor as yourself."

I'd guess most of us could quote the phrase by memory, "love your neighbor as yourself." It's right up there with "do to others as you would have them do to you." Our familiarity might cause it to lose some of its profound significance. This is yet another reality we have in common with Paul's original readers.

With the charge to express freedom through love, Paul affirms this directive from the Law.

Wait... the Law?

*I thought his whole point was that we are **not** under the Law. Has this entire thing been leading up to a big bait-and-switch? Not cool, Paul! Not cool.*

All along, the Law included directives like this. It was, after all, God's Law. It makes sense that it would have goodness and kindness embedded in it. If we go all the way back to Leviticus 19:18, we read this "love your neighbor as yourself" phrase for the first time. It comes after a litany of laws centering around how to treat each other. (Read Leviticus 19:9-18 for the full reference.)

In spite of the hullabaloo Paul makes about the Law's inadequacy, Old Testament passages like this remind us of the heart of the Law. That, at its core, it was designed toward community with God and other people. Over time, its trajectory shifted toward attaining righteousness.

Full disclosure: That was a grossly oversimplified description of the Law. I admit it. It's not commentary-worthy. Or even bumper sticker worthy. But... if it crystalizes even one intention in you toward loving others from a place of freedom, it's worth it.

See, the thread of humanity's existence from the beginning of it all, including the Jewish Law, is God's love. So it makes sense that freedom enabled through grace unleashes us to "love our neighbor" in a way that the Law never could. Because pure love... God-given love... is not offered out of obligation but given through grace. And Galatians reminds us that only through Jesus are we free to give that kind of love.

Describe love that is born out of freedom.

When it comes to the directive to love, we always have a choice. When we choose, out of freedom, to act with love toward our "neighbor," we are perpetuating life both in ourselves and in the person to whom we are expressing love.

$$\text{Grace} \rightarrow \text{Freedom} \rightarrow \text{Love} \rightarrow \text{Life}$$

Yet, out of that same freedom, we could choose to withhold love or act non-lovingly. With that, we choose to squelch the spiritual life. Boiling it down, we reinforce the trajectory of sin, which at its most extreme is death itself. Every time we settle for less than love, we are giving sin power over us. And the more we do that, the stronger its hold becomes. So, although Christ freed us from death, we find ourselves still choosing to live that way.

$$\text{Grace} \rightarrow \text{Freedom} \rightarrow \text{Non-Love} \rightarrow \text{Death}$$

Dramatic much?
I admit. It sounds dramatic. And it is. But also ... it isn't.

Remember: Because Jesus's sacrifice was enough to eternally remove the threat of death, we don't need to worry that too much sin will remove grace. Much of our Galatians discussion so far has cemented the "enough-ness" of Jesus' death and resurrection on our behalf. I hope you have come to a place of fully believing that. So, if we know grace is sufficient and eternal, then we must know that our post-grace choices can't remove grace.

But they certainly must have *some* impact on us! And that's what Paul is getting at here.

Ponder these two trajectories for a few minutes.

$$\text{Grace} \rightarrow \text{Freedom} \rightarrow \text{Love} \rightarrow \text{Life}$$
$$\text{Grace} \rightarrow \text{Freedom} \rightarrow \text{Non-Love} \rightarrow \text{Death}$$

Embrace the Undoing

What additional thoughts or feelings come to the surface for you as you think about these trajectories in your own choices?

Where does your spiritual bling fit into the equation? Listen intentionally for what God might say to you about this.

Our choices toward love or not, in the context of our freedom, cannot diminish the grace we've received. Solely founded in Jesus, grace is enough regardless of our choices. Which path we choose, though, profoundly affects how we experience Christ today...and every day moving forward.

In the end, there is still an outward mark of a believer, but it's no longer circumcision. Now the mark is love. When we exhibit this sign of faith—love in the midst of our freedom—we are no longer distracted by our own sparkle. Instead, we are transformed.

It's right about then that we hear an unfamiliar sound, like metal bits hitting the floor.

Oh...it must be the rest of our bling falling off.

Chapter 18

A Tale of Two Days

On Monday I drove the Volt. The heated leather seat welcomed me into the warm, cozy car that had been preparing itself for my arrival by automatically running the heat. Something I told it to do with the app on my phone. The Volt connected with said phone, and I watched with delight as the dashboard screen lit up with a mirror image of my phone screen. Calls, texts, maps, music... all right there at my fingertips.

As I backed out of the driveway, I didn't even have to turn my head. The backup camera had me covered. I could see 180 degrees out the back of my car. I sped down the street feeling like the stealthy queen of the road that I am. Throughout the day, I simply told my Volt where I wanted to go, and it told me how to get there. When a call came through, the environmental controls automatically turned down the fan... because who can enjoy a conversation with all that air blowing? And hours later, when the sun finally set, the instrument panel adjusted its brightness to allow for maximum viewing pleasure.

After driving all over town, I pulled into my garage and glanced down at the instrument panel that informed me I still had eight electric miles remaining until the Volt would start using gas. Wow... the earth must love me! I walked back into the house as my car automatically locked itself and waited patiently for my return the next day.

But the next day, I drove the Van.

The Van is 13 years old. It's the paid-off clunker that sits in front of our house. It gathers a nice layer of dirt while it waits for one of us to drive it because we have an armchair to move or a group of kids to haul around. I got in the Van, relieved it started on the first try. I turned on the radio and then reached over to the glove box to retrieve the adapter cord we use to connect the phone to the Van. The connection sprang to life with a loud crackling, then simmered down to just a background buzz that never went away.

A few minutes into my drive, the windows started to fog, but the defrost was acting up, so I rolled the windows down. Luckily that cleared things in just a few minutes, but as I went to roll the windows back up, the passenger window decided not to cooperate. It rose two inches, then laughed at me. Well, in truth, it just rattled, but it definitely felt to me like it was laughing. Determined to get my to-do list done, I continued on, ignoring the wind … and then rain (Did I mention it started raining?) blasting through the open window. I tried answering a call, but who can enjoy a conversation with all that air blowing?

After my last errand, I backed out of my parking spot, craning my neck to check all angles, but still managed to hit the median that I couldn't see behind me. A little worse for wear, I eventually returned the Van to its place at the curb in front of our house. As I got out, my sweater snagged on the tear in the seat's vinyl. Distracted, I fumbled for my keys to lock up and forgot to turn off the headlights. I walked back into the house as the Van's battery began its slow death … that I wouldn't discover until next time.

The Van versus the Volt. Two options each day. My choice. I have the freedom every day to choose which vehicle I'll drive. And inevitably, that particular vehicle characterizes a lot of what my day looks like. Efficient, streamlined, and modern, or inconvenient, clunky, and frustrating.

Choice is a powerful thing. We make countless choices throughout our day, each one slightly altering our experience for that day (or even for many days to come). I don't spend much time thinking about how cool it is that I *get* to make choices. I mostly think about the choices themselves. For a moment, let's step back from our action-taking, decision-surplus-ness existence and consider how incredible it is that we have the power to choose!

List 5-10 things you get to choose every day. Try to include both significant and insignificant choices.

The list could go on and on. We choose what we'll wear, what we'll eat, what street we will take to a particular place, what we will say, what projects we will work on when, what shows we will watch, what we will read, what we will post on social media, when we will do a chore, how often we will drink a glass of water. There is no shortage of choice for most of us.

The first four chapters of Galatians focus on freedom—how we got it, why we have it, and how we sometimes forget about it. Moving into the last two chapters, Paul begins to describe the implications of that freedom on our choice.

Our choice centers around two very different vehicles that carry us through our day. Read Galatians 5:16-18 and identify our two options.

> *16 So I say, walk by the Spirit, and you will not gratify the desires of the flesh. 17 For the flesh desires what is contrary to the Spirit, and the Spirit what is contrary to the flesh. They are in conflict with each other, so that you are not to do whatever you want. 18 But if you are led by the Spirit, you are not under the law.*

Embrace the Undoing

This passage says that _____ and _____ are in conflict with each other.

How would you describe "Spirit"?

How would you describe "flesh"?

The word used for Spirit is *pneuma*. It specifically refers to the Holy Spirit. One disclaimer about *pneuma* is that it is "never referred to as a depersonalized force."[6] In other words, it's associated with the person of God. Not as just some unknowable force.

The Spirit desires us to be led by and to walk with the Spirit.

"Flesh" is the Greek word *sarx*. *Pneuma* in this passage is utterly divine. *Sarx* is utterly human: Our physical bodies, our human desires, or tendency toward selfishness and self-preservation. Animal instinct at its core.

But, what *pneuma*/Spirit and *sarx*/flesh have in common is that both are personified. The Spirit is a personification of God. The flesh is how we are personified as humans.

What does it look like when two people have opposing desires? Describe what kinds of things happen when two people want very different outcomes in a given situation.

---

6 "Search for: Galatians 5:16 – Strong's Interlinear Bible Search - Reference Desk." *StudyLight.org*, www.studylight.org/desk/interlinear.cgi?ref=47005016.

Now imagine the two in conflict are your "flesh" and God's Spirit. What does that look like?

In another letter, Paul writes, "I want to do what is right, but I can't. I want to do what is good, but I don't. I don't want to do what is wrong, but I do it anyway" (Romans 7:18b-19, NLT). In what ways do you relate to Paul's description of the struggle?

Here's where we get back to choice. Freedom gives us the choice of which "person" will win. The freedom Paul's been writing about for four chapters doesn't mean God wins the battle of desires going on in us. It means that we have the **choice** about how we will live our lives: following our own flesh or following the Spirit.

Paul has made the point that Jesus' work on the cross covers us in grace and is enough, in and of itself, to fully reconcile our relationship with God. So the old Law, the rituals, the religious practices, and the markers of who is spiritual and who is not are no longer tied to salvation. We are free from the compulsion to perform.

With this in mind, finish this statement in your own words: Freedom is...

Thinking about your flesh and the Spirit being in conflict with each other, write down some specific areas or situations in your life where you are experiencing this conflict.

In what areas or types of conflict does your flesh usually win? For example, do you have a hard time controlling your words? Are you indulging in unhealthy habits you know are hurting you or others? What physical temptations often get the best of you? Is there a grudge you can't release? Do you withhold love in order to get your way? What comes to mind for you as you consider where your flesh "wins."

Where does God's Spirit tend to win?

The freedom God gives us is a radical move on His part. He made it possible by sacrificing everything, yet He does not require anything from us except belief. He gives grace as an unearned gift, and freedom is like the instructions on how to use that gift. Whether we choose to let the Spirit or our own desires rule our life, it doesn't change the reality that we still get the gift.

What our choices **do** change is how our life will be characterized. Following the Spirit produces life-giving outcomes. Choosing the flesh leads to destruction. Paul goes into graphic detail about these two very different results. He describes the trajectory of our freedom … for good or for bad.

The Message paraphrase puts it this way:

16-18 My counsel is this: Live freely, animated and motivated by God's Spirit. Then you won't feed the compulsions of selfishness. For there is a root of sinful self-interest in us that is at odds with a free spirit, just as the free spirit is incompatible with selfishness. These two ways of life are antithetical, so that you cannot live at times one way and at times another way according to how you feel on any given day (Galatians 5:16-18).

What do you hear the Spirit saying to you in these words?

What would change for you if you lived "freely, animated and motivated by God's Spirit"?

Freedom is not what makes us live a good life. Freedom is what enables us to choose how we will live our life—in submission to sin or in submission to the Spirit.

Creative Challenge:
As a tangible way to remind yourself about the spiritual choice we explored today, find or make something to place in a visible spot in your car for this week. Let it spark an awareness of the God of freedom who empowers you with choice. Ask yourself whether you are driving the Van or the Volt in that moment. The Van, so like our flesh, with its broken, unreliable, frustrating outcomes. The Volt, like the Spirit, with its intuitive, comforting, protective essence. Be intentional in your freedom to choose what's best moving forward.

Chapter 19

Pace Yourself

Having given some thought to the struggle between the "flesh" and the "Spirit," read Galatians 5:24-25.

24 Those who belong to Christ Jesus have crucified the flesh with its passions and desires. 25 Since we live by the Spirit, let us keep in step with the Spirit.

Picture keeping in step with the Spirit. In what ways is that difficult for you?

When I visualize my attempt to stay in step with the Spirit, vivid episodes flash in my memory. The pictures aren't of a spiritual nature. There is nothing remotely divine about them. When I imagine what a battle like this is like, I think of dogs. Three dogs, to be exact.

Tat, my brother's Bullmastiff, lived with us for a while during my elementary years. Tat was a 120-pound drool machine with the pull equivalent of a small tractor. Grabbing the leash one boring day, I was met with wide but droopy eyes and an overactive tail. I confidently clipped the leash to his collar which, buckled in the last hole, barely made it around the girth of his neck. Nanoseconds after the door latch unclicked, Tat was full steam ahead. I made an honorable attempt to be the alpha dog, as they say, but that's hard to do when his head is bigger than your torso, and he's forgotten all about you and the measly leash pretending to control him.

Something popped in my shoulder, and my arm ripped off. (Well, not exactly, but the pain told me otherwise.) With adrenaline kicking in, I managed to wrangle Tat back toward the front door. Our walk was very short-lived. We only made it to the mailbox.

Keeping in step is hard to do.

Dog episode #2 involved Lady, the first dog that was ever truly *mine*. I met her when I was seven and she was seven weeks. The name alone has an air of class. Lady. She would never be so rude as to dismember me. But all the manners in the world weren't enough to enable her to read my mind.

One fall day, deciding to take dog-walking up a notch, I opted to ride my bike with Lady running alongside. I'd seen it done. How hard could it be? My messy ponytail danced in the wind to the beat of Lady's claws tapping the sidewalk. *I'm a genius!*

The telephone pole grew out of the sidewalk like a tree with no branches. I wasn't fazed by the quickly shrinking distance between me and said pole. The only thought my 4th-grade mind offered was to simply ride around it. Which is, in fact, the right answer. My error was neglecting to factor in the bike, the leash, and the furry creature running tandem.

Her canine brain similarly formed the thought to go around the pole.

Unfortunately, it was the *other side* of the pole.

I don't remember what happened after that.

Keeping in step is hard to do.

As an adult, my first dog was an English Bulldog named Boo, named for her ghost-like fur and her Halloween birthday. This breed is not known for long walks. Or for any propensity toward activity. In dog shows, bulldogs are in a category called "non-sporting breeds," the only category marked by what the dogs *don't* do. They are literally defined by their lack of exercise. Boo enjoyed a leisurely walk to the end of the block and back once every two weeks.

One day, for a change of scenery, we drove to a local forest preserve to enjoy the walking trail. The Midwest trees were in full cooperation, releasing their October leaves to the forest floor. The cool breeze outpaced us as we meandered down the path. Boo was more active than usual. Jogging ahead in short spurts to sniff a tree. Zig-zagging off the trail to follow a bird or a sound.

The leash's retracting cord buzzed mechanically, adjusting to Boo's constant movement. Until that moment when it clicked and jerked my arm backwards, letting me know the cord was fully extended. I tugged. Nothing. Tugged again. Nothing.

I turned to see Boo sitting amidst a smattering of leaves. Her bloodshot eyes unresponsive to my leash pulls.

"I'm done," she said. (I don't speak dog, but her body language communicated very clearly.)

It was as if her exercise timer went off, instantly taking her from playful dogness to utter immobility. On the other end of the leash, I pulled like a tug-of-war champion, but she reacted as if a tiny thread was suggesting she move. Nothing.

Did I mention bulldogs are stubborn? Their dog show category could easily be called "non-cooperative."

The standoff (sit-off) ended with me pushing her from behind to a standing position. We walked at a snail's pace back to the car, and she slept the rest of the day.

Keeping in step is hard to do.

With dogs, we *know* whether or not we are in step. We can see it clearly and adjust as needed. Throughout our day, we adjust our stride to other humans, too: walking in a group, driving on a freeway, playing on a team. We simply look around and respond to the movement around us. But pacing ourselves gets tricky when we can't simply "look around."

Keeping pace with the Holy Spirit is doubly challenging. The Spirit is relational *and* invisible... two attributes that make it difficult to simply look around and adjust. I want to keep in step with the Spirit, as Paul encourages, but how do I know it's working? Paul helps us out here. He spends the rest of the chapter familiarizing us with indicators.

Think of these indicators as seeable gauges for spiritual realities. They are noticeable actions, habits, tendencies, and outcomes able to reveal where your steps are aligned—with your flesh or with the Spirit. Sit with these indicators for a few minutes as you read Galatians 5:19-24 (NLT).

> *19 When you follow the desires of your sinful nature, the results are very clear: sexual immorality, impurity, lustful pleasures, 20 idolatry, sorcery, hostility, quarreling, jealousy, outbursts of anger, selfish ambition, dissension, division, 21 envy, drunkenness, wild parties, and other sins like these. Let me tell you again, as I have before, that anyone living that sort of life will not inherit the Kingdom of God. 22 But the Holy Spirit produces this kind of fruit in our lives: love, joy, peace, patience, kindness, goodness, faithfulness, 23 gentleness, and self-control. There is no law against these things! 24 Those who belong to Christ Jesus have nailed the passions and desires of their sinful nature to his cross and crucified them there.*

This passage is a description of indicators disguised as a list. And just like most lists—especially biblical ones—we come to it with some baggage. Our auto-response kicks in as we reach for the proverbial Sharpie to decorate the list with impressive checkmarks. Peace. Self-control. Gentleness. Check. Check. Check. No envy. No impurity. No rage. Check. Check. Check.

But wait... didn't Paul spend the entire book of Galatians until now destroying the whole notion of religious lists? Certainly, he's not imploding the very faith structure he took five chapters to construct! Quite the opposite. He wants the reader to view this listy passage *with* the context of everything he's written so far, to embrace these descriptions as indicators that a Jesus-follower is living in love.

We can connect the dots this way. "These character qualities are not a new list of laws or moral codes that must be kept; they are the result of living and being led by the Spirit."[7] When our lives are characterized by love, joy, peace, and all the rest, we are walking in the Spirit. Conversely, when our lives are exhibiting immorality, jealousy, hatred, and all the rest, we are not walking with the Spirit.

What (if anything) changes for you as you receive these verses, not as behavioral obligations but as indicators showing your connection to the Spirit? How does this relate to your understanding of freedom in Christ?

I'll admit, sometimes I still get tripped up with the line "those who live like this will not inherit the kingdom of God" (Galatians 5:21). It sure sounds like it's saying that if these negative attributes characterize our lives, we will be cut off from eternal life with God. But does this sound like Paul to you? Of course not. So what is he really saying?

Context is key. In Jewish teaching, "kingdom of heaven" or "kingdom of God" was not typically understood as relating to the afterlife. It was used as a statement of God's rule.[8] In other words,

---

7 "Freedom for Moral Transformation (5:22-26)." *The IVP New Testament Commentary Series*, by D. Stuart Briscoe et al., InterVarsity Press, 1990.
8 "Galatians 5:16-26: Living by the Spirit." *The Jewish Annotated New Testament: New Revised Standard Version Bible Translation*, by Amy-Jill Levine and Marc Zvi Brettler, Oxford University Press, 2017, p. 385.

not inheriting the kingdom of God means not experiencing God's rule in your life. The phrase is *descriptive* not *prescriptive*. It describes what happens in the present when you live this way. You miss out on the manifestation of the Spirit in your life.

Romans 14:17 describes the kingdom saying, "… the kingdom of God is not food and drink but righteousness and peace and joy in the Holy Spirit." Applying these words of Paul in Romans to Galatians 5:21, we understand that our sinful behavior hinders us from experiencing the outcomes of life in the Spirit.

And here we find ourselves back at freedom… freedom to find our spiritual security in Christ's work, not our work (or lack thereof).

When we view this passage as a guide for choosing love instead of a do-and-don't-do list, we gain insight into how in step with the Spirit we are. It's not a recipe for good-Christian-ness, it's a picture of life with the Spirit. We may be tempted to disregard that seemingly subtle difference, but let's not underestimate how much this new perspective shifts our vest-decorating trajectory.

If we respond to these verses as accomplishments to strive for, we will continue to amass bling bit by bit, quickly falling back into old spiritual habits. But if we are convinced of Jesus' full grace—enough for all our missteps and more—we're free to choose the way of love as an authentic response to this grace. When we choose love (described in verse 22), it is an expression of our love for God and others. We receive His love, and we return that love by way of loving our neighbor. It's "faith expressing itself through love" (Galatians 5:6).

Remember, though, that in our freedom, we are free to choose. So when we are not in step with the Spirit, our actions are characterized by the descriptions in verses 19-21. While these choices affect our experience of the Spirit, they don't change our standing of full acceptance through grace. And that means, while the godly choices don't give us any "credit," the negative choices don't condemn us.

Praise God!

Spend a few minutes calling to mind your personal journey through Galatians to this point. Talk with God about the specific ways He has spoken to you about freedom—from performance, from striving, from earning, or from self-aggrandizing checklists. What do you sense God is saying to you now about receiving His grace regardless of your behavior or choices?

Re-read Galatians 5:19-24 (possibly in several different Bible translations) and consider what "indicators" you see in your life lately. What does this mean for you in terms of walking in step with the Spirit?

Thinking about your own tendencies away from love, what personal indicators could you add to Paul's list that reveal you are not in step with the Spirit?

On the flip side, what additional indicators do you notice that reveal you are walking toward love, in step with the Spirit?

Read the following excerpt from a commentary on this passage. Pay attention to the word pictures it paints and spend a few minutes praying for a more consistent response to the Spirit's life in you.

"The Spirit sets the line and the pace for us to follow. Keeping in step with the Spirit takes active concentration and discipline of the whole person. We constantly see many alternative paths to follow; we reject them to follow the Spirit. We constantly hear other drummers who want to quicken or slow down our pace; we tune them out to listen only to the Spirit."[9]

---

9 "Freedom for Moral Transformation (5:22-26)." *The IVP New Testament Commentary Series*, by D. Stuart Briscoe et al., InterVarsity Press, 1990.

Chapter 20

The Three C's (Part 1)

Clutching the railing that ran the perimeter of the cruise ship, I huddled in the ice-cold breeze, amazed I was on an Alaskan cruise. Everywhere I looked, picture-perfect views. A casual camera click in any direction resulted in postcard-worthy shots. Simply majestic.

It was my first cruise, and I leaned into all the stereotypes: gorging at dinner, enthusiastically touring each port, and attending every show they offered. One bit of entertainment was a series of lectures by a naturalist who had lived in, studied, and explored Alaska for the better part of 40 years. Okay, so maybe not "entertainment" per se. More like education. But I will say he was highly entertaining, so that must count for something. He painted verbal pictures of his adventures with whales, sea lions, and eagles. But the most memorable presentation by far was the one about bears. Specifically, the part about how to not get eaten by one.

"First, you must be familiar with the signs that a bear might be ready to attack."

Yes, I want to know that. Seems important.

"If the bear is looking you in the eye, with his head low…"

OK, check. No eye contact. Watch for sinking head.

"…and if his ears are back, and the fur on his neck is standing on end…"

Wait. What? How close do you think I am to this bear? If I can see the hair on the back of its neck, aren't I ... like ... already dead?

"Now that you know what to look for, let me tell you what to do."

I'm ready, pen in hand. I'm taking notes.

"You've probably heard the advice to play dead. That's good advice ... if it's a brown bear. Especially if it's a mama brown bear, play dead. Lay flat on the ground. Stay as still as you can. Be prepared to stay that way for a few hours."

Hours?

"I've had to do that before. I came across a Mama Bear, and I got down and lay very still. She watched me for a while to make sure I was really dead. After 20 minutes or so, she walked toward me, put her two front paws on my back, and pressed (grunt) ... pressed (grunt) ... pressed (grunt).

That must have killed! She's gotta weigh over a hundred pounds.

"Then, all 400 pounds of her ... "

Four hundred pounds! How are you NOT dead?

" ... sauntered back over to her spot, where she watched me some more. Just to make sure I was really dead."

Uh ... yeah ...

"Then after another half hour or so, she padded my way, placed her paws on my back, and pressed (grunt) ... pressed (grunt) ... pressed (grunt) again!"

Seriously, Dude, how are you not dead?

"This went on for over an hour, back and forth. Finally satisfied that I was dead, she wandered away."

This isn't helping me. I feel so much worse about my bear danger prowess than I did before I got here.

He then went on to explain that if you come across a black bear, however, you should not play dead. That's the last thing you want to do.

OK. I guess this is helpful. Brown bear: play dead. Black bear: do not play dead. Good thing I know the difference between brown and black.

But there was one more nugget of wilderness wisdom yet to unfold. Guess what? A brown bear can be brown or black and a black bear can be black or brown.

What? You've got to be kidding me!

He continued with his "helpful" advice. "There are other distinctive traits between a black and brown bear. For example, the shape of their noses, the back of their necks, and the size of their claws."

Again... how close do you think I am to this bear? If I'm within range to comparatively rank claw size, then I know the answer. The answer is I'M DEAD!

And this is why I stayed on the ship, indulging in the bottomless nacho bar instead of trekking through the Alaskan wilderness like some kind of bear bait. Wildlife rules are just too complicated. Do this. Don't do that. Black is brown. Sometimes.

But even with all that, here's one thing I know, and I think you know it, too. It's easier to respond correctly to bears than to humans. Especially when we are confronted with their sin. (The human beings, not the bears.) The next section in Galatians has specific insight into this. So, let's pay close attention as we consider our response to other people's sin.

Before reading the passage, take a few minutes to pray for openness and insight for what God might say to you. Then consider your tendencies when it comes to responding to others when you believe they are sinning. Do you have a need to be right? How strong is your desire to correct others? How would you describe your thoughts and feelings in these situations?

We are each predisposed toward a mindset that comes with us into our relationships. It's those tendencies you reflected on a moment ago. They are ingrained in deep, subtle ways. They can skew even our best intentions for an appropriate response to the wrong we see in others.

But a secret lies in the juxtaposition of the two phrases in this passage. If we understand the wisdom and warning embedded in the words, it can change the dynamic of some of our most difficult interactions. In fact, how well we apply this advice will affect every relationship, every conversation. Let's get to it...

Read Galatians 5:25-6:5.
25 Since we live by the Spirit, let us keep in step with the Spirit. 26 Let us not become conceited, provoking and envying each other. 1 Brothers and sisters, if someone is caught in a sin, you who live by the Spirit should restore that person gently. But watch yourselves, or you also may be tempted. 2 Carry each other's burdens, and in this way you will fulfill the law of Christ. 3 If anyone thinks they are something when they are not, they deceive themselves. 4 Each one should test their own actions. Then they can take pride in themselves alone, without comparing themselves to someone else, 5 for each one should carry their own load.

Read the passage again, and write any thoughts or prompts that come to mind.

These verses paint a vivid picture of the Galatian church we have been getting to know. The conflict surrounding how their faith *should* be expressed led to conceit, envy, temptation, deceit, and comparison (just to name a few specifically listed in the passage). They were on a destructive trajectory that Paul attempts to correct.

To better understand it and to more clearly identify our own, let's break it down.

We've already learned that some of the Jewish converts proposed that certain practices of the Law were still necessary. Imagine yourself as one of these believers. You sincerely think it is good and right to observe these practices. They matter. They are important.

How would you feel about those who decided not to follow these parameters? What would you think about their faith?

It's shockingly easy to get into the minds of the Jewish converts or at least to make a pretty good guess. Because we know our own thoughts when we see an incongruity between what someone says they believe and how they live. On its simplest level, this is how it must have been for the Jewish converts. It starts with noticing the difference. Then it evolves into more.

Stage One: Comparison. Oh, that dreaded word. The mental place where nothing is good enough and all things are offensive. The place where we can't win, but we keep going there. Our eyes become our enemy, and the mirror becomes more about perception than reality. For good and for bad. Comparison is tricky that way.

With faith, comparison becomes a beauty pageant for blinged-out vests.

"Look at my shiny, baubly faith! My vest hardly has any room on it, it's so full of all the things. What about you? Oh. Huh. Your vest is missing some key decorations. Where are your sequined patches? Did you not sew them on yet?"

Immediate but subtle conclusion: I win at the faith competition.

Stage Two: Conceit. Call it pride. Name it arrogance. Dub it ego. It's "I'm better than you."

Stage Three: Correction. Stemming from what feels like obedience, we pursue the underwhelming vest owner. We diligently get them back "on track."

"Here's what you should do... Let me tell you how to fix this... fix you. Start doing this. Stop doing this. I'll draw the boxes for you, and you check them off as you go. We'll do this together. I'll be your self-appointed faith coach. Together, we'll get that vest in shape in no time."

It's a rush of pious adrenaline. Not only do you get credit for your obedience in reaching out to this fallen fellow Christian, but you'll get bonus points when they clean up their act and point to you as their savior.

What begins with the briefest flash of comparison quickly develops into the conceit that manifests in corrective efforts to make a kingdom difference.

Those three words—comparison, conceit, and correction—are heavy with meaning with which most of us are all too familiar. Spend time listening for anything God might have for you as you ponder your own experience with the three C's.

Here's a "real-life" example of the three C's in action. By real life, I mean that it plays out this way in real life, but I use quotation marks because it's not actually from real life. I'm making this up. Quotation marks let you get away with anything. I'm taking full advantage.

A "Real-Life" Example.

Renee is checking all the boxes, faith-wise. She is at church every week, sometimes twice. She serves in the Children's Ministry.

She reads her Bible through in a year ... every year. She leads a Bible study in her home and writes the curriculum herself. She's been on 22 mission trips and donated anonymously to the outreach program. Renee's vest is super blinged-out!

She recently heard sad news about Sydney, a woman who volunteers with her in the toddler classroom on Sundays. Sydney's husband left her. When Renee heard this, her heart simply broke. She wanted to help in any way she could and reached out to invite Sydney to coffee.

"Thanks for meeting with me," a hollow-eyed Sydney said.

"Of course," Renee countered. "I'm so sorry you're going through this. I just can't imagine. I want to help in any way I can."

"That means so much to me."

"Do you want to tell me more about what happened?"

"Okay."

Amidst tears and whispers, Sydney unfolded her story. Her whole story. Exactly 18 minutes into her telling, a shift began to happen in Renee.

Sydney confessed that her husband left because of an affair. One she had. This was the second time. After the first one, they stayed together, but the crack in their marriage widened, and she didn't know how to fix it. She pushed down the feelings of inadequacy, but it was just a Band-Aid. Although she had been sober for three and a half years, when the shame and guilt reappeared, so did the drinking. Ultimately, it's what made room for the second infidelity. After that, her husband was done.

Initially, Renee entered into Sydney's mess with soft-hearted compassion. As the bigger story was revealed, her compassion fizzled away. The story of bad choices, selfishness, and sin. And the inevitable consequences of each. In the listening, Renee arrived at a conclusion that left no room for compassion. Here was a woman who brought this mess on herself.

The pattern of comparison—conceit—correction played out in Renee. Comparison is a no-brainer; of course she would compare. In her mind, it might go like this:

I can't believe you would ruin your marriage like that. And after getting a second chance. My marriage isn't perfect, but at least I've been faithful. Sure, I indulge sometimes… maybe desserts or a sweet, frothy coffee drink, but it's not an addiction.

Renee's proverbial nose inches a tad higher as comparison arrives at conceit.

You call yourself a Christian? You're acting nothing like a true follower of Jesus. It's not always easy for me, but I manage to walk the talk, and you know what? I'm doing pretty good at it. Anyone who knows me would say the same.

Spiritual arrogance and a look-what-a-super-Christian-I-am pride have no other recourse than to fix the not-so-super Christians all around them. As if with a resigned sigh, pride tells arrogance, "It's up to us again. We'll clean up this mess."

Another slight shift happens in Renee. Born out of a little bit of pity and a generous helping of embarrassment that her fellow Jesus-follower is failing so badly, a decision is made to correct Sydney. The rules come easily for Renee (because she's so good at following them… if you weren't sure on that, she'll be the first to remind you). She sets to work coaching Sydney on what to do and what not to do to get her faith back on track. Let the correcting begin!

Correcting feels like the right choice at the time, but is it the loving, good, and wise choice? Award-winning author, pastor, and all-around leadership guru John Maxwell says, "Are we going to spend our lives connecting with people or correcting them?"[10]

---

10 Maxwell, John C. Global Leadership Summit, 2016, Monticello, Crossroads Church of Monticello.

Maybe on some level you can relate to Renee. Describe a situation or relationship where you have exhibited comparison, conceit, and/or correction. Consider your verbal and non-verbal responses that have revealed those tendencies in you. Take your time and reflect honestly. Be as specific as possible.

Reflecting on the passage again (Galatians 5:25-6:5), in light of your personal example, what response do you sense God is asking from you?

An honest inventory of our failings (in this case, our comparison, conceit, and/or correction) can elicit feelings of shame. We might feel unworthy or stupid, asking *why do I get stuck in these patterns?* If those emotions surface and threaten to distract you from what God is revealing, take time to talk with God about it. Remember that He knows you and loves you unconditionally. He is not disappointed in you. His grace is real and thorough.

Our propensity toward the three Cs and our willingness to identify them is an important part of embracing the rich wisdom found in this passage (Galatians 5:25-6:5). While it may be easier to play dead when we have trouble navigating the three Cs, our discipline to face them with authenticity moves us closer to truly being a Jesus-centered community.

Chapter 21

The Three C's (Part 2)

Now that we've identified the three C pattern in the passage (comparison, conceit, and correction), we have a context in which to receive the rest of the wisdom Paul includes in the passage. Re-familiarize yourself with Galatians 5:25-6:5.

> *25 Since we live by the Spirit, let us keep in step with the Spirit. 26 Let us not become conceited, provoking and envying each other. 1 Brothers and sisters, if someone is caught in a sin, you who live by the Spirit should restore that person gently. But watch yourselves, or you also may be tempted. 2 Carry each other's burdens, and in this way you will fulfill the law of Christ. 3 If anyone thinks they are something when they are not, they deceive themselves. 4 Each one should test their own actions. Then they can take pride in themselves alone, without comparing themselves to someone else, 5 for each one should carry their own load.*

Each sentence in this part of Galatians has the potential to speak life into whatever situation you are facing right now. In light of that, I encourage you to take time to consider Paul's words—sentence by sentence—and listen for what God might have for you.

Embrace the Undoing

In the space below, write your understanding of the verse/sentence listed. Take as much time as you need. Allow room for God to get your attention in the specific and personal way that only He can. Think of this as less of a chart to be completed and more as a tool to pay attention to where God might be leading you. Be willing to follow where God leads you.

Verses	What you think it means. What questions it elicits. What images it evokes.
25 Since we live by the Spirit, let us keep in step with the Spirit.	
26 Let us not become conceited, provoking and envying each other.	
1 Brothers and sisters, if someone is caught in a sin, you who live by the Spirit should restore that person gently.	
1b But watch yourselves, or you also may be tempted.	
2 Carry each other's burdens, and in this way you will fulfill the law of Christ.	
3 If anyone thinks they are something when they are not, they deceive themselves.	

4 Each one should test their own actions.	
4b Then they can take pride in themselves alone, without comparing themselves to someone else, 5 for each one should carry their own load.	

Look back over your comments. Do you see a theme? What response do you have to what came to mind during the exercise? Note any specific action you feel prompted to take.

In my own reflection on this passage, one word used twice caught my attention. Verses two and five contain the word "carry," but in very different contexts. The first phrase is "carry each other's burdens." The second time, "each one should carry their own load." I've read this passage many times over the years, but I never noticed the dichotomy of those two phrases until recently.

Carry each other's burdens.

Carry your own load.

Which is it? Do we carry the burdens of those around us? Is that living in community? Or do we each carry our own load? Does God expect that of me? If I'm supposed to carry my own load, how can I also expect someone else to help me with it? And what are these loads and burdens anyway?

In this part of Paul's letter, he is instructing on the careful navigation of restoring one who has sinned. The text implies that two dynamics are occurring simultaneously along the way. Think of it like two parallel paths. The first path is helping restore someone after they have failed; the second path is checking our own heart in the process.

In regard to the first—helping restore someone—Paul uses the phrase "carry each other's burdens" (Galatians 6:2). Come alongside a struggler to share the weight of their burden. Do it under the guidance of the Spirit—"walk in step with the Spirit" (Galatians 5:25). Do it with gentleness. When you do, you will "fulfill the law of Christ" (Galatians 6:2).

As for the second path—the one where we look inward to our own motivations and mindset—Paul reminds us that the burden we must personally bear is to be responsible for our response to the sin. Do we become conceited because we compare our tame sin to another person's more blatant sin? We are warned to watch ourselves, not think we are better than we are, and test our own actions. There is a responsibility on our part to check our heart. That is the load that each of us must carry ourselves.

This sentiment is hinted at toward the end of verse one when Paul writes, "But watch yourselves, or you may also be tempted." Tempted to do what? The temptation isn't that we might fall into the same sin as the person we are trying to restore. The temptation is that while we are helping them, we would become conceited and arrogant in our own self-righteousness.

Remember: two parallel paths. We walk one path alongside another as we gently restore them. We walk the other path in our own heart, checking for the three C's (comparison, conceit, correction).

Thinking back to Renee's story in the previous chapter, the concern is not that Renee might be tempted to, like Sydney, cheat on her husband or become an addict. Her temptation (brought on by her exposure to Sydney's failures) is that she might think too highly of herself in comparison. For Renee, "carry each other's burden" means she lovingly, gently helps Sydney restore her faith. "Carry your own load" means that as Renee does so, she is careful not to become puffed up, self-aggrandized or haughty. Renee's burden—her responsibility—is to be mindful that her response to Sydney's sin does not become sinful itself.

This idea is reiterated in a different way at the end of verse four. It says to "take pride in [ourselves] alone." Take pride in the fact that you are watching out for your own tendencies toward arrogance. This is a good type of pride, not the dangerous pride that results when we think we are better than we are.

We carry each other's load when we respond with love to their sin. But as we do, there is a load of our own we must carry. It's the responsibility on our part to eliminate comparison, judgment, and self-righteousness.

Take a moment to clarify your thoughts. In your own words write out how you understand the two paths of carrying your own burden while carrying someone else's, too.

One practice that diminishes our tendency toward the three C's is to regularly make ourselves aware of our own sin. This process might reveal truths about us that increase our compassion for others. It might lower our defenses and make room for the Holy Spirit to provide insight to our own shortcomings. The more honest and thorough we are in identifying our trouble spots, the more fully we are freed up to express God's love to others.

Humility is bolstered through an honest inventory of our own struggles and failures. This kind of humility counteracts conceit. Think through (and write down if you are comfortable doing so) your areas of struggle/sin/failure.

Spend time in prayer, thanking God for His forgiveness and continued restoration in these areas of your life.

Galatians 6:1 instructs us to restore gently. The Greek phrasing used here implies the setting of a broken bone. While not painless, it requires things like gentleness, patience, and follow through. What could restoring gently look like for you?

As you check your heart in the area of correction, ask God to reveal to you if embracing humility and helpfulness might require an apology from you. Take time to honestly reflect on how you may have misstepped in your efforts to correct someone else.

These are hard lessons. Checking our motives is not only humbling but complicated and often fuzzy. Walking with the Spirit means walking alongside invisible footsteps. But faith tells us they're there, and grace surrounds every stumble (whether ours first or ours when we've succumbed to pride when helping someone in their stumble). So, keep walking. The reward is closer than you think.

Chapter 22

Spiritual Seeds, Diamond Rings, and Buggy Boulders

Thoughtfully read these next Galatians verses.

> *7 God will never be mocked! For what you plant will always be the very thing you harvest. 8 The harvest you reap reveals the seed that was planted. If you plant the corrupt seeds of self-life into this natural realm, you can expect to experience a harvest of corruption. If you plant the good seeds of Spirit-life you will reap the beautiful fruits that grow from the everlasting life of the Spirit* (Galatians 6:7-8, TPT).

From all we've discovered so far, consider what these verses are saying to you. What circumstance, habit or aspect of your life connects with this passage? With that in mind, rewrite this passage in your own words.

Read what you wrote. Take a moment to pay attention to how the Spirit might be stirring in you. Write any reflections you feel prompted to explore.

Embrace the Undoing

"You reap what you sow," shouts out from these verses. Sowing a Spirit-seed brings drastically different results than sowing a self-seed. The harvest shows up in all sorts of ways. Sometimes it's in the consequences of our decisions or our ability to enjoy healthy relationships. It might be in how we feel about ourselves or how we process both pain and joy.

Because we are "vest" people who are prone to be intrigued by spiritual bling, the harvest we most easily notice is external, visible to ourselves and others. Easily categorized as good or bad. But the harvest that's harder to identify is that which internally connects us more closely to Jesus.

Sowing seeds of Spirit-life results in a deeper experience of Jesus in our day-to-day lives. And when we are connected to Jesus, we are empowered to live freely and fully. "While it is absolutely true that our grounds of acceptance is the sacrifice Jesus Christ made on our behalf, *our connection to that sacrifice* is by way of a faith that works itself out in the many good works in a person's life."[11]

How does your seed-sowing relate to how connected you feel to Jesus?

Connectedness to Jesus is a difference maker! Especially when we don't immediately see the results of the good we have done. Let's face it…our acts of love and goodness don't always provide immediate payoff. *Most* don't. Some reading this right now are wading through an unfairly long waiting period between the good that's done and any noticeable positive outcome. Paul speaks to that in Galatians 6:9.

> *So let's not get tired of doing what is good. At just the right time we will reap a harvest of blessing if we don't give up* (NLT).

---

11 "Galatians 6:7-10." *NIV Application Commentary*, by Scot McKnight, Zondervan Academic, 1995.

(We can read those words and think, "Who determines 'just the right time'? Must be God's timetable, not mine." And that's true. But God's timetable is the trustworthy one.)

I recently heard a true story that uniquely illustrates this verse. Back in 2004, 84-year-old Mary Grams was busily weeding the garden on her family farm. Down on her knees, in the dirt as any good gardener would be, something caught her eye. Or should I say *didn't* catch her eye? She glanced at her hand. Instead of seeing the sparkle of her wedding ring, she saw nothing. No ring! All weeding stopped while she frantically dug through the surrounding dirt, looking for her ring. No luck.

Mary decided to keep this news from her husband, buying a similar-looking cubic zirconia ring to replace it. Apparently, he didn't notice. Shocking. She did confide in her adult son, telling him of the long-gone ring.

Thirteen years passed. Mary no longer lived on the farm but it stayed in the family under the care of her son and his wife. One afternoon, Mary's daughter-in-law, Colleen, began to think about dinner options and headed to the garden to harvest a few fresh vegetables for a salad. She piled them next to the kitchen sink and began cleaning, peeling, and slicing. She came across a very unusual carrot. In her dripping hands, Colleen held a short, gnarled carrot, its middle cinched tight by a gold band studded with multiple diamonds.

At 97 years old, Mary finally got her ring back!

Like Mary's diamond ring, our goodness and love can lay in the proverbial dirt, giving us nothing to show for a harvest. Maybe it's the tough love you've had to show to your child. Maybe it's a thousand kindnesses toward a prickly acquaintance. It might be your earnest prayers on behalf of someone else. Or the loving sacrifices that are unappreciated.

God encourages us to keep at it! To unreservedly bring love into our relationships and world, even when it seems to be for nothing.

Embrace the Undoing

Somewhere deep in someone's soul, roots are growing into or around the love that was sown.

What love-induced sowing have you done that has yet to produce a tangible harvest?

What disappointment have you felt as a result? Talk to God about this disappointment and listen for His response.

Sometimes the most wearying, disappointing sowing is into the hearts of other people of faith. It can be so hard to love Christians. This must have been true even back in the early church. Paul writes:

> *Therefore, as we have opportunity, let us do good to all people, especially to those who belong to the family of believers* (Galatians 6:10).

This added note of specific encouragement to *especially* do good to other believers speaks to the antidote to the three Cs (comparison, conceit, and correction). When my faith doesn't look like yours, when you don't appear to be taking your faith seriously enough, when you have messy, offensive habits, when you continue to make the same poor choices again and again ... what will my response be to you? Will I keep sowing my diamonds of goodness even if they get buried in your dirty soil?

"Generosity is the hallmark of a spiritually alive person."[12] Life in the Spirit empowers me to be generous with my love.

---

[12] "Galatians 6." *The Bible Panorama*, by Gerard Chrispin, Day One Publications, 2005.

When the Spirit is working in me (producing outcomes like the fruit of the Spirit noted in Galatians 5:22), I am more likely to have a healthy detachment from my "good deeds." I know they are the Spirit in me, not something that gives me bonus points with God. This goodness, born of the Spirit in me, is a conduit of God's love to others. And I can freely—generously—offer that love, knowing that God's love for me is unchanged whether I do or not.

The choice to love is mine every moment of every day. I can liberally give goodness away because I am freed from the compulsion to hoard it for myself like a deposit in my God account. This is the life of freedom God's grace grants me.

Remember back to an instance when you felt big generosity with your love, possibly even moved by the Spirit to love well. What did you inwardly experience as you felt compelled to give? How do you think God was present with you in that gift of love?

Several years ago I found myself at a women's retreat in the Southern California mountains. The retreat center was nestled in a valley between two ridges, cutting us off from the rest of civilization. (And by that I mean there was no cell phone service.) Without technological distractions after the main session, we were invited to the dreaded time of "solitude and silence."

For an extrovert like me, this invitation was less welcome than a plantar wart, but as I mentioned at the beginning of this book, I'm a people-pleaser. My tendency morphs into rule-following. So off I went. *By myself.*

I aimlessly circled around and up the backside of the camp on an unfamiliar walking path. I wanted to find just the right spot for this all-important alone time with Jesus, so I kept walking... and walking. After fifteen minutes, my anxiety transitioned from *what am I going to do with thirty minutes alone... er... I mean, with Jesus* to *I'd better find a place to sit right now or I'll fail the assignment!* Just as I committed to stopping at the next possible place, I came to an iron gate on which hung a dusty, rusty "Do Not Enter" sign.

Now what?

Sighing, I turned around, determined to sit on the first surface I spotted. A few steps away sat a rock with a flat surface... but the surface was at a 45-degree angle, and it culminated in a sharp granite edge. But the team told me Jesus was waiting, so what was I supposed to do? I sat. At a 45-degree angle.

This better be good, Jesus.

My flip-flops crunched the dry weeds at the base of the rock, and a bug crawled up my ankle. The sun focused all its attention on me, and eye-stinging sweat dripped through my eyebrow.

Anytime, Jesus. I'm ready to be wowed.

In the retreat folder I found the "alone time" Bible verse and came across the words "dwell in the land and enjoy safe pasture" (Psalm 37:3). I shifted my position because the rock was poking my rear end, and I laughed at the irony that my current "land" was neither dwellable or pasture-like. It was dry. Dusty. Forgotten.

Not unlike how I had felt lately.

Life with God felt shallow, and disappointments—the most glaring of which was a recent miscarriage—bubbled under the surface.

I looked up from the page, and my eyes scanned the terrain across the valley. I faced a mountainside lush with a deep green forest. Though I was miles from it, I could sense the coolness of the earth below the tree blanket. It was still, as if anticipating my gaze.

I brought my head back down to where I sat on the uncomfortably sloped rock.

I thought, "Here I am in this barren land but, God, I feel You calling me to the lush mountain. I'm settling for lifelessness when You offer me fullness. Help me say yes to Your invitation to the life-giving pasture."

In that moment, I saw a real-life picture of what a fully grace-covered and fully free life entails. Richness beyond measure, limited by my own resistance to life in the Spirit.

And therein lies the heart of what Paul has been addressing in these last two Galatians chapters: as Jesus-followers, fully dependent on the work of the cross for unchanging acceptance by God, our daily experience of a faith-driven life is greatly affected by our free choice to live in the Spirit or in the flesh.

The choice to reside on the lush mountain or remain on the bleak side of the valley is before us at all times. The life-work of the Spirit is ever-ready to manifest itself in conjunction with how we live out our freedom. The Good News Bible version of Galatians 6:8 speaks of us planting seeds in two fields: one of natural desires and one of the Spirit. There are so many ways to describe the duality of our life in freedom.

Flesh or Spirit.

Death or life.

Lush or desolate.

My way or God's way.

When I've opted for God's way, I catch a peek of how my Creator intended it to be. The realization triggers a waterfall of gratitude for a God who loves us so much that He would design a way back to Him, secured through the cross, and glimpsed in the moments where I choose life.

Think about the ways you will choose life today. Being specific about your situations, describe how you may have walked in the flesh until now but how you can intentionally choose to walk in the Spirit going forward.

Chapter 23

Grace Enough

I'm writing this chapter while sitting in a local coffee house in a small town 30 miles from home. It's down the road from the high school where my daughter is none-too-happily enduring the SAT exam, number 2 pencils and an old-school calculator in hand. I wouldn't trade places with her for all the cronuts in the world.

Sitting among the mismatched chairs, I'm sure I'm the only non-local at House Beans. Coffee is served in mugs that were bought at the artisan street market which I detoured around on my way to SAT drop-off. Specialty drinks are poured with the precision of a brain surgeon... but one who makes leaf decorations out of oat milk and other non-dairy substitutes. Customers enter with by-name greetings from the barista.

One local orders a mocha "for here" and two minutes later the behind-the-counter hipster hands her a short clear glass filled with the chocolate liquid. When I say "filled" I mean filled! To the brim. If a speck of air-dust were to waft onto the surface of the drink I'm confident it would have caused it to spill over the edge. So full.

The customer grips the hot glass in both hands and begins the long walk across the shop. I watch as she stills her entire body—statue level still—except for her Birkenstocked feet, which take tiny, baby-penguin steps to protect her liquid treasure. Her eyes remain intensely glued to the frothy liquid. Her only goal is to keep it safe.

Embrace the Undoing

I'm sure I see a drizzle of anxiety-induced sweat drip down the side of her cheek.

Why won't she simply take a sip to alleviate the fullness? It's torture watching the molasses pace of the mocha transport. Hours later (feels like), she arrives at her destination, gently placing the glass on her table.

I can feel the exhale. *Is it mine or hers?* Her whole body relaxes. Success. Glass still ridiculously full. I'm struck by the intense hyper-focus of a woman and her coffee. Her cup, so very full, absorbing all her attention.

This scene played out before me like a real-life picture of grace and me. Grace: filling every micro-space of my spiritual existence; Me: solely attuned to protecting its fullness and priority. At least, I hope so.

After spending years immersed in Galatians with Paul's treatise on the sufficient fullness of grace, I've gained a proverbial inch toward a deeper embrace of grace. I have learned a great deal but am simultaneously aware I've barely begun. Just one inch deeper but so very significant. In that inch, I've gained confidence in God's acceptance of me, apart from anything good or bad that I do. My eyes have been opened to the limitless freedom I have because Jesus already gave me everything I need for life with Him. The generous gift of grace is so full that even one speck of "works" would make it spill out messily and ruin the artistry God made. The performance is simply not needed. I am already made new.

Galatians 6:14-15 (Good News Translation) reinforces the outcome of grace in our lives.

> *14 As for me, however, I will boast only about the cross of our Lord Jesus Christ; for by means of his cross the world is dead to me, and I am dead to the world. 15 It does not matter at all whether or not one is circumcised; what does matter is being a new creature.*

How does this passage echo and strengthen your own trajectory toward a deeper understanding of the sufficiency of grace?

One commentary elaborates on being a new creature, describing the transformation as "the birth of the spirit in the heart."[13] Does that phrase evoke a picture in your mind's eye? The Spirit being born in the heart of a person. Each believer's Spirit "birth day." The event, the process, and the journey of the Spirit's life taking up residence in the heart of a Jesus-follower.

It's the mark of grace on each of us.

The Spirit's relentless residency.

This gift of the Spirit is characterized by a certain done-ness that is based on the Spirit, not us. Such security! And it is our reality. Paul speaks elsewhere in his writings of the Spirit as a "seal."

> *20 For no matter how many promises God has made, they are 'Yes' in Christ. And so through him the 'Amen' is spoken by us to the glory of God. 21 Now it is God who makes both us and you stand firm in Christ. He anointed us, 22 set his seal of ownership on us, and put his Spirit in our hearts as a deposit, guaranteeing what is to come* (2 Corinthians 1:20-22).

> *13 And you also were included in Christ when you heard the message of truth, the gospel of your salvation. When you believed, you were marked in him with a seal, the promised Holy Spirit, 14 who is a deposit guaranteeing our inheritance until the redemption of those who are God's possession—to the praise of his glory* (Ephesians 1:13-14).

---

13 "Commentary on Galatians 6." *The Expositor's Greek Testament*, by William Robertson Nicoll, M.A., L.L.D., 1960.

As you ponder these verses, how is your security in the work of the Father, the Son, and the Spirit strengthened? What does it mean to you that you are "sealed" by the Spirit?

We started our journey recognizing that some undoing needs to get done! Like the recipients of Paul's letter, we have a habit of adding on to grace. It's as if the Spirit is born in us, empowering this new life, and we set the Spirit aside and say, "Watch what I can do!" During this journey, we have peeled back our efforts and accomplishments, layer by layer, to reveal the sterling perfection of Christ alone.

Enough. Always enough.

This is where we find freedom. Freedom because grace is enough. Our mocha mugs are filled to the brim. There's simply nothing we can add that's worth anything at all in the category of grace. The compulsion is released, and in its place are the actions of new life bubbling up, but this time, it is from a place of freedom. We *get* to live this way. We choose it.

Imagine your cup filled with grace. Not one bit of space unused. Spend a few minutes expressing gratitude for what this has meant in your life. Have a conversation with God about what it means for what's next.

Notice the death language in verse 14. Many translations say the world is "crucified" to me and I to it. It's helpful to think of "world" as "the way of the world" as in our *flesh*, our self-striving inclination. I like the Good News Translation which offers this phrasing, "... the world is dead to me, and I am dead to the world." The way it used to be—my dependence on my flesh—is totally over.

If I had my own Bible translation, I'd write, "We pronounce a big ol' 'You're dead to me' to the trappings of performance."

And why is that? How can this be? Simple: the cross. Our freedom journey starts at the cross (and we must keep referring back to the cross) because the cross represents death itself. But it's a death that no longer hangs over us as inevitable. Through the resurrection, Jesus' experience of the cross redefined death as only a temporary state, and it conquered the very power that death used to hold over us. What used to be our permanent future can now be the state of our dependence on our flesh: Dead.

Paul wisely reminds us that our only boast—our only credit or checkbox—is what was done *for* us. In light of that, what matters is the new creation we have become. You might not always feel (or even act) like a new creation, but it is what is true about you.

Chapter 24

Rule of Life

Can we just breathe for a sec? Yeah... a full, deep breath. Let the gravity of grace and its eternal enoughness dive deep into your lungs and permeate every last bit of you. We've inched our way through Galatians. Sometimes one word at a time, often with complicated callbacks to Old Testament ritual, always with the desire to more fully align ourselves with the richness of this thing called grace. So we find ourselves at the end with two words we simply cannot overlook.

Galatians 6:16 says, "Peace and mercy to all who follow this rule..."

Peace and mercy. Let's start with peace. What comes to mind with that word? The Greek word *eirēnē* used in this verse offers several nuances of peace. The word represents anything from national tranquility to harmony between individuals to safety and security to the Messiah's way of peace to an assurance of salvation to the state of someone after death.

Phew! That's a lot of peace-angles. So many aspects of meaning for such a small word. Which one applies in Galatians? I say, let's own them all!

Grammar nerds, consider yourself warned: run-on sentence coming at you...

The Messiah's way allows me as a follower, a believer, to be assured of my salvation while also being empowered to reconcile with others because we are all one in Christ, and as each of us do that more and more, we can permeate our families, churches, cities, countries, and even our world with the tranquility that comes through Jesus, all the while experiencing my own sense of safety and security founded on who I am through Christ and what my eternal trajectory is, so that at the end of my life I am confident that unending peace will be mine when I dwell with God forever.

Double phew!

What if we lived in that breadth of peace every day? I imagine it would change so much of how we experience life with God. It would quiet our inner critic. It would soften the pull toward impressing others and performing for God. True peace leaves us resting confidently, secure in what Christ has done for us.

Take a moment to imagine your day marked by peace. What would your work, conversations, thoughts, relationships, and choices look like? Then talk with God about your desires related to peace.

We know our souls resonate with peace. We were created to live in it, after all. Something... well... *peaceful* settles over us when we imagine a peace-filled life. But, in an ironic twist, just when we visualize peace being real for us, an almost immediate doubt asks, "Will I ever truly live in that kind of peace?"

To that lingering question, Paul inserts one more word in his closing thoughts: Mercy.

I'm a Gen-Xer, which means that by default I have to love Karate Kid. Okay, maybe love is not required. I get that not all of us in my generation are fans, but most of us can at least admit we have been affected by the 1984 Blockbuster. If you've ever uttered the phrase "wax on, wax off"... If you've ever used the word "miagi" as a verb as in "He really Miagie'd that problem" ... If you've ever heard yourself shout "sweep the leg!" in a moment of feigned desperation, then you too have been impacted by this beloved movie.

But there's one phrase, a slogan really, that you might only be able to quote if you are a true fan: "Strike First. Strike Hard. No Mercy." The ethos of the hyper-aggressive, testosterone-laden, ultra-competitive dojo of Sensei John Kreese. He demands his students yell this in response to the "motivational pep talk" he is shouting at them while 2.5 inches away from their faces. He's drilling it into them. His students never let up or show compassion. His students never give others a soft landing. They strike with everything they've got. They train their inner monster toward a zero percent chance of going easy on their opponent. No. Mercy.

But with Jesus, we get all the mercy.

I've heard mercy described as "not giving the punishment that is due." It's a compassionate holding back of deserved punishment. Think back to the gruesome animal carcass halves story of Abraham we talked about earlier. Do you remember the part where God—materialized as fire—floated through the path between the dead animals? Do you remember how it was *only* God who did? It was a foreshadowing. Failure to be true to the covenant would not dissolve the covenant. Instead, God Himself would take the punishment on our behalf to uphold the covenant promise. Mercy displayed through the cross.

Paul calls the Galatians to a life of peace in all the ways. Peace is the goal. Mercy, then, is the compassionate response of God when we miss the goal.

How have you seen God's mercy in your life?

Getting very specific, how have you experienced God's mercy in the last 24 hours?

These two words *peace* and *mercy* are offered to those who "follow this rule." Does anyone else find it odd that Paul throws in this word "rule"? After so much focus on lessening the hold of the Law and embracing grace, it's ironic he would entreat them to live by a rule. This is no mistake on Paul's part. He has done everything he can to tell his readers that the compulsive law-keeping and check-listing is not the way of Christ and that as new creations, we are released to live Spirit-led. This is the new *rule*, if you will.

The word for "rule" metaphorically means a standard, but it literally means a straight piece of wood used to keep straight whatever is attached to it. All of Galatians explores the spiritual reality that keeps us aligned with God: grace received then lived out in love. Remember, true freedom is not found by living however you want. Freedom simply means we have the choice between walking in the flesh or walking in the Spirit, and when we choose the Spirit, we experience a day/week/year/life filled with grace and love.

And for us far-from-perfect humans who regularly make the unwise choice, there is mercy again and again because grace is based on Jesus' work, not our performance.

Take a few minutes to talk with God about how you are experiencing (or not experiencing) alignment to this "rule" Paul describes. Is there an area where peace is lacking or where mercy is needed? Listen for what God might be saying to you.

Confession is not my favorite thing to do. You? I'm guessing the same. Admitting to a friend I'm wrong, even in small instances, is like swallowing that bite you took that was too big, but now it's in your mouth, and by sheer determination, it'll get down your throat, but it kind of just sticks there creating a pressure that's not supposed to be there, and it impedes your breathing so you gulp water, and for a second it's worse, and then finally it's done.

I hate being wrong. If we can simply "move on" without having to state my mistake out loud, yes, please! *Let's skip the admission. We both know I'm wrong. We'll pretend this never happened. I love your shoes. Are they new?*

This avoidance habit, though, robs me of the chance to receive grace from my friend. It removes the moment where compassion, understanding, and forgiveness could have been given. It steals the opportunity for me to more deeply experience my friend's acceptance of me... flaws and all. If this is true of my human relationships, how much more so with God?

It's when we face our misalignment with the "rule" that we grow in awareness of the vastness of God's grace. The about-to-spill-over-mocha. It's served to us by the Creator Savior, who did everything to make it real and asks us to believe it. Jesus + nothing. As we experience the ongoing gift of grace, we live into our beloved belonging. We wrap our hearts around the confounding truth that we are fully accepted by a perfect God without strings attached. Only belief. No performance, no earning, no impressing, no bling.

When you think about your relationship with grace, what hinders you (in any way) from experiencing its fullness?

Embrace the Undoing

Picture the vest once again. Imagine all that you've attached to it. Notice what bubbles up in you (emotion, a memory, an image of God, a physical sensation, a verse). What do you hear God saying to you?

We all have ways we try to add to grace, to "decorate the vest" as we live out our faith. As you've read this book, I trust you and God have dialogued about this. And be prepared... the conversation will be ongoing. Isn't that, after all, what a relationship is? In this relationship, every time you unpin a decoration, you'll gain another sweet encounter with the gift of grace.

So to you who wander away from walking with the Spirit, struggle to set aside your spiritual achievements, compare and find others lacking, have gotten good at being good, work to be worthy of belonging, perform your way to pleasing God, check off the Christian to-do list with permanent marker, keep score, or crowd your vest with shiny baubles... I say, embrace the undoing because grace will always be enough.

Notes

1. "Initial Reception of the Spirit (Galatians 3:1-2)." *The IVP New Testament Commentary Series*, by D. Stuart Briscoe et al., InterVarsity Press, 1990.
2. "Miracles by the Spirit (Galatians 3:4-5)." *The IVP New Testament Commentary Series*, by D. Stuart Briscoe et al., InterVarsity Press, 1990.
3. "Galatians 3:29." *Jewish Annotated New Testament*, by Amy-Jill Levine, Oxford University Press, 2017.
4. "New Spiritual Relationships in Christ (3:26-27)." *The IVP New Testament Commentary Series*, by D. Stuart Briscoe et al., InterVarsity Press, 1990.
5. "Galatians 4:21-31." *New Testament Commentary Series*, by D. A. Carson, Inter-Varsity Press, 2007.
6. "Search for: Galatians 5:16 – Strong's Interlinear Bible Search - Reference Desk." *StudyLight.org*, www.studylight.org/desk/interlinear.cgi?ref=47005016.
7. "Freedom for Moral Transformation (5:22-26)." *The IVP New Testament Commentary Series*, by D. Stuart Briscoe et al., InterVarsity Press, 1990.
8. "Galatians 5:16-26: Living by the Spirit." *The Jewish Annotated New Testament: New Revised Standard Version Bible Translation*, by Amy-Jill Levine and Marc Zvi Brettler, Oxford University Press, 2017, p. 385.

9. "Freedom for Moral Transformation (5:22-26)." *The IVP New Testament Commentary Series*, by D. Stuart Briscoe et al., InterVarsity Press, 1990.
10. Maxwell, John C. Global Leadership Summit, 2016, Monticello, Crossroads Church of Monticello.
11. "Galatians 6:7-10." *NIV Application Commentary*, by Scot McKnight, Zondervan Academic, 1995.
12. "Galatians 6." *The Bible Panorama*, by Gerard Chrispin, Day One Publications, 2005.
13. "Commentary on Galatians 6." *The Expositor's Greek Testament*, by William Robertson Nicoll, M.A., L.L.D., 1960. (Galatians 6:15). Frederic Rendall.
14. "What Was the Purpose of the Law (Galatians 3:19-20)?" *The IVP New Testament Commentary Series*, by D. Stuart Briscoe et al., InterVarsity Press, 1990.

A Word of Thanks...

This book was a long time coming due to my unfailing commitment to procrastination and my determined efforts to never let a distraction go unnoticed. Along the way of my much-too-long journey of birthing this book, my faithful companions continued to cheer me on!

First, I want to thank my agent Cynthia Ruchti at Books & Such Literary Management. Your patience and kindness as you held my hand through this writing process has been astounding. I'm pretty sure you wrote and published several books of your own in the months you waited for even one more chapter from me. Did I mention your patience? You strategized with creativity, and you pivoted with me when needed. I can only guess that I'm your least productive client, but you always treat me as if I'm the best. Thank you for bringing your excellent insights to this project. It quite literally wouldn't have happened without you. I'm so grateful God brought you into my life and you were willing to take a chance on me.

Thanks, too, to the rest of the team at Books & Such for being so life-giving. Special shout out to Jill Kemerer who joined this project in the 11th hour in order to take it to the finish line. Your way of managing logistics and details took me from overwhelmed to confident in our very first conversation.

Thank you to my small group of friends who gave helpful and honest feedback on each and every chapter. Cindy Anderson, Emily Nelson, Jodi Harris, and Kristen Meek, you bolstered me and believed in me with every comment, question and debate about comma placement. Way to be awesome!

Thanks to my writer's circle with West Coast Christian Writers. You were a safe place to begin exploring the concept of this book. You were honest, welcoming and affirming. My early experiences in the group laid a solid foundation that allowed me to bring this project to completion.

Thank you Liana Moisescu for creating a cover that so beautifully represents the message of the book.

Thank you, Chris, Quinn and Kennedy for being my biggest cheerleaders. My writing has interrupted evenings, weekends and vacations... but I only ever felt support from you three. You're all my favorite.

About the Author

Andrea Coli is a pastor, speaker and author who has been in ministry for over 25 years. She is passionate about affirming and activating female ministry leaders and is a founder and the Executive Director of Lead Bold, a leadership community for women in ministry. She is the Teaching Pastor at CrossWinds Church in California's Bay Area and is a member of the Teaching Team for Preacher Chicks United, an incubator for women of color to cultivate their gifts of preaching and teaching. She loves connecting with women leaders and serves as pastoral lead over the Women's Network of Transforming the Bay with Christ.

Andrea received her masters degree from Fuller Theological Seminary then counter-balanced her Bible smarts by moving to Las Vegas where she had the once-in-a-lifetime opportunity to join Second City's cast of an all-improvised show. She talks about this experience in her book *Scriptless: What I Learned About God on the Las Vegas Strip*. With a background in improv comedy and degree in theology, she has a unique perspective that takes her readers on a journey from out-loud laughs to moments of tender truth.

Andrea and her husband Chris have the privilege of raising two (almost) grown daughters. In her spare time she thinks about how she wishes she had more spare time. You can find her at www.andreacolispeaks.com or connect with her on social media at @andreacolispeaks and @leadingbold.

www.ingramcontent.com/pod-product-compliance
Lightning Source LLC
Chambersburg PA
CBHW070150100426
42743CB00013B/2869